Triumph
Over Tears

Triumph
Over Tears

Mary Brite

THOMAS NELSON PUBLISHERS
Nashville   New York

Library of Congress Cataloging in Publication Data

Brite, Mary.
   Triumph over tears.

   1. Widows—Religious life. I. Title.
BV4528.B74   248'.843   78-27107
ISBN 0-8407-5680-1

To Vi Fickel, Bea Greiner, Gretchen Kenny, and the Solitaires who have shared with me; to Rev. Keith Cook and the congregation of the Presbyterian Church of the Master; to my earthly father Leo Bowers, who by example helped me understand and rest on my heavenly Father's Word; and to my "now" husband Bob Brite, who lends me constant support and encouragement.

Table of Contents

Preface

I don't know when I have come upon a book as readable and specifically practical as this one. It was difficult to put it down even though the subject would usually be thought of as depressing.

The title of this book, *Triumph Over Tears,* is very descriptive of Mary Brite's own ability to enjoy God-given triumph over what could have become a deep bitterness caused by her own sad losses. She does not minimize the negatives, but one certainly senses a pervading background of Christian hope in every subject discussed.

Mary Brite and all her widow friends who are quoted have the ring of credibility. This is an authoritative book. It is exactly the way things are. Nothing is covered up or hushed up; it is not a wallowing in "Isn't it awful?"

Perhaps most important—the author has done

something specific about solving some of the problems of widowhood that she is addressing. She has been successful in showing others how it is possible to organize groups of widows for their own education, growth, and encouragement.

It is exciting to believe in the very real possibility of replicating her model with similar groups all across the country. She is not suggesting something too difficult to reproduce. It is all so simple and sensible that we wonder why someone hasn't thought of this loving, helpful approach to widows long ago.

Her model of widows' groups comes at just the right time when service societies and local congregations of Catholics, Protestants, and Jews are seeking better ways to give the faith more human and loving dimensions. We hope the study of this book by task forces will result in hundreds of such groups being formed.

Granger E. Westberg

President
Wholistic Health Centers Inc.
Hinsdale, Illinois
November 1978

Acknowledgments

My gratitude to Jeanette Collins, Bev O'Brien, Rev. Keith Cook, Rev. Norman Hagley, Dr. Beverley Mead, Sally Orr, Connie Turner, Joan Lineback, to my editors for constructive criticism and helpful comments; and to Marjorie Dohse for final draft typing—several times.

Triumph
Over Tears

Introduction

I watched the flashing lights on our rented
Cessna 205 as it took my husband off into the
twilight on New Year's Day, 1967.

I found his body in the wrecked fuselage five
hours later.

While adjusting to widowhood and rearing four
children alone,* I searched for a reply to my eternal
"Why?"

As a result of my childhood training, it was natural for me to seek that answer in the Scriptures. The
answer proved to be more eternal than the question. An informed lay couple spent many hours with
me because they believed James 1:27: "Pure religion and undefiled before God and the Father is

---

*This story is told in *Top of the Valley*, published by Warner
Press, 1976.

this, To visit the fatherless and widows in their affliction, and to keep himself unspotted from the world."

Under their guidance I found assurance that my tragic circumstances were something God allowed rather than caused. I realized that my favorite verse was still valid; Romans 8:28 says, "We know that all things work together for good to them that love God. . . ."

Instead of just reading and reciting Scripture about Jesus as my Savior, I invited Him into my life to become my *personal* Lord and Friend. I emerged from this chrysalis stage no longer a crawling caterpillar wondering *who* I am, but a soaring butterfly knowing *whose* I am.

As God's child I know peace and joy and appreciate His undeserved support and strength. As I become obedient, I respond to the command to help others. He prepared me through experience to assist widows, and it is a rewarding ministry.

He caused other widows to share their feelings with me and then encouraged me by His Spirit to urge you, too, to kneel down with each widow, to help her lift and carry her particular burden.

What Christ Jesus has taught me I seek to share with you.

> *"They say time will heal the heart, and it does, a minute at a time."*
> —Comment made at a Solitaires meeting

1

Help Me, Please

Anne's telephone call came in the middle of the morning. Like other widows, she found holidays hard to handle emotionally, and it was affecting her physically.

"Hello. Brite's."

"Hello, Mary. Is that you?"

"Yes."

"This is Anne.* I need someone to talk to—I'm so upset. I can't even get out of bed today."

"I'm sorry, Anne." I could hear her crying.

"Nothing is right since Tom died. Tomorrow is Christmas and tonight I have company coming for dinner and I—I just don't want to live anymore."

Although I have been visiting with widows for

---

*Names of widows have been changed throughout to protect their privacy.

ten years, I was momentarily thunderstruck when Anne said she didn't want to continue living.

My first thought was that her future might depend on what I said in the next few minutes. It was good to be able to say, "I know how you feel," and to know that she knew I spoke the truth.

My mind was racing ahead, groping for something to say. We had been together several times and visited in a group with other widows. She had often cried during our first meetings, but during the last two months she had seemed beyond that stage. What had upset her? I reviewed my first Christmas as a widow, years ago. What made me feel good? Company.

"Is Tommy there with you?" Tommy was her fourteen-year-old son. Months earlier we had discussed Anne's need to stay well and care for him since she was his only remaining parent.

"Yes, and I feel guilty about it, but I asked him to just squeeze me as hard as he could this morning, so maybe I could feel something."

"Don't allow guilt to smother you, Anne. Can you think of anything at all you'd like to do?"

"No. I need to make cookies and finish wrapping gifts—but I just can't face any of that today!" The sound of her sobbing brought tears to my own eyes. My throat tightened.

"Would your older son and his family come for dinner?"

"I don't know. They always have before, but he just ignores me now. He won't call and let me know. I hate to call him all the time."

I didn't know how much she relied on God,

although I knew she had appreciated inspiration from a priest who spoke at our last widows' group meeting. From long experience I knew this was not the time for Christian clichés.

I had learned to pray while I listened, knowing that "with God all things are possible" (Mark 10:27). *I* couldn't prevent her from committing suicide, but I knew *He* could. So I asked the Lord Jesus to speak the right words through me to steady Anne.

"Can you think what upset you?" I asked. I learned she had attended a funeral the week before, and it had stirred up memories of her husband's death. She agreed to try once more to get up and start her day's work. She would call back during lunchtime to report what she had accomplished.

Promptly at noon, Anne called.

"Well, I'm feeling a little bit better," she said. She explained that her daughter was sick and had asked her to take care of the grandchildren. So Anne was babysitting and making cookies.

We talked again ten days later. Anne shared her fears.

"I need money for food. . . I have to find a job. . . I'm not trained for any special work. . . I can hardly get dressed and out of the house for interviews."

"Anne, would you be interested in a cleaning job?" I asked.

"I can't find enough energy to clean my own house. How could I possibly do it for anyone else?" she replied.

I should have known, I thought to myself. I

19

recall feeling as hollow and useless as a deserted snake skin.

Later, as I analyzed my conversation with Anne, I renewed my resolve to keep aid to widows balanced on three sides of the triangle: physical, mental, and spiritual. You may think I listed those in the wrong order, but in practice they work best that way most of the time. Frequently it is necessary to build a friendship and work to a position where I've earned the right to spotlight my viewpoint.

Physical life is important, but spiritual life is inexhaustibly significant. I like to share—especially with widows—what my personal relationship with the Lord means to me: a deep assurance that He is in control, now and eternally. I am pleased when I can share insight on any phase of adjustment with any widow, as we have much to experience.

Milly and I met because her brother attends my church. We discussed one aspect of a widow's new knowledge.

"I did something I really didn't want to do," she said hesitantly. "I went to a Christmas party with people in the office where my husband used to work." Her voice broke and tears interrupted the conversation.

"Why did you do that?" I questioned.

There was a comfortable silence until she regained her composure.

"I felt I owed it to the group, although none of them have bothered to visit me since John died. I knew they didn't know what to say to me, but it made me angry anyway." She found another tissue and wiped her eyes. "An unexpected benefit came from that experience. I found out that they all felt bad about John's death." She forced a weak smile.

"Did they say so?"

"No. I just knew from being with them that they were sorry and it gave me a good feeling."

"So you're glad you went?" I asked.

"Oh, yes! The shoe is on the other foot now, though. A man who works near me is dying just like John was, and it's terrible. I'm just like everyone else. I don't know what to say to him."

"Don't you think it would be a relief for him to have the subject of death out in the open with at least one friend?"

"Well, maybe, if he's ready. I'll try to talk to him about it. But I might end up crying."

"We've talked about that and have decided it isn't anything to be ashamed of—remember?" I gently reminded Milly.

"That's right. I'll have to try to work toward that." Milly assumed an assertiveness and agreed it helps in adjusting if you can recognize your problem.

Why do women feel completely out of place once they are widowed?

For one thing, our society is so couple-oriented that even a woman temporarily without her husband for a social evening feels some discomfort. It's as if someone says, "Choose up sides." Both teams are selected and the game begins—leaving one standing there, left over. We blame our society when divorced, widowed, and single people feel ostracized. Since our society includes you and me, we are the logical ones to change it. An old saying applies well here: "If you decide to change the world, begin at home."

Maybe the widow feels more alone and left out than she really is; perhaps she is just as acceptable as ever. But the large number of widows who disagree with that statement may indicate a factual basis for their belief that they no longer belong.

I have known only one widow who kept several couples as close friends and continued in her usual social group. I don't know how she did it. I do know it wasn't easy. She was formerly shy and her friends were surprised when she became outgoing after her self-assured husband died. She invited couples to her home for dinner and carried complete responsibility for hospitality. She kept her theater tickets and enjoyed dramatic productions with the group. She is to be admired.

Some widows feel reluctant to go out anywhere. Betty shared the following story:

"After Jim died, I just wanted to stay in the house all the time. The chore I hated most was grocery shopping. Jim and I had bought food together for years. He would choose the meat and I would get everything else. After he was gone, I'd see other couples together in the store and it really upset me."

"How did you overcome that?" I asked.

"A new neighbor moved in. She really pulled me out of it." Her eyes misted over as she remembered. "That lady called me up one day. 'We are going to a garage sale,' she said. I told her I had a headache and felt sick so I couldn't go.

"A few minutes later she knocked on my front door. 'Come on,' she said, 'We're going.'

" 'I feel sick. I can't go,' I insisted. She dragged me out the front door. Then I sat down on the front steps and started crying.

"She went inside my house and brought a cold, wet washcloth from my bathroom. 'Here, wash your face. We *are* going,' she said again."

"How long was that after Jim died?" I asked.

"It was a *year*. I told her when we got to the car that I still felt sick and I couldn't go. But she said she'd bring me home if I got worse. So I went. It was good for me and helped me get over the worst time. Later she took me to the grocery store and shopped with me several times."

Widows may be partially aware that they aren't adjusting well, and wish to change. The presence of psychological fences doesn't mean they'll blow away with the next blustery wind. Grief problems grow giant-sized because women have refused to think of themselves in any connection with death before; therefore, they have never considered what naturally surrounds it.

A widow unexpectedly left with ten children willingly accepted a questionnaire concerning her adjustment, then kept it six months. When she finally returned it to me she explained, "I've been widowed seven years. As I tried to answer this, I realized I'm not the only person feeling the way I do. The questions made me see I hadn't progressed very well. I had to do something to improve myself and my actions—and my relationship with my children—before I could return it to you. I'm much better now."

Such a confession affirms the value of facing facts regarding death. Articles and books on this topic help us understand ourselves and our reactions, which leads to mental and physical well-being. For widows it is late, but we can still learn.

And as soon as we learn, the Lord calls us to put our knowledge to good use, to reach out and touch others with His love. I hear Him saying, "Do you love Me?"

"Yes, you know I do."

"Feed my sheep."*

A great part of "feeding widows" is helping them understand themselves. Good feeding provides energy and courage.

Eileen shared the following positive experience with our group. We were trying to think of particularly helpful actions people had taken to aid us in adjusting.

"About a month after Galen died, a friend mailed me a bright red box. It said EILEEN'S SMILE BOX on the outside and was about the size of a cigar box. There was a smiling face on the outside. Inside were bright squares of construction paper and each had a handwritten message."

"What did they say?" one of our group asked.

"They were all quick and easy to read, and to the point. One I still remember said, 'Life, like the Bactrian camel, has two humps—one to carry the burdens of yesterday, and the other, the hopes of tomorrow.' I think that quote was by William Walter DeBolt. Some were by Norman Vincent Peale.

---

*Paraphrased from John 21:16.

That was the nicest thing anyone did for me when I was first widowed. Anyone could make one of those boxes."

Eileen was usually rather quiet, but she became excited as she described the way her friend had shared not only her time, but a portion of herself. She wanted to pass along the kindness shown her, and so later she gave a shopping bag full of good used clothing to a financially strained younger widow.

It may not work to push a lot of positive thinking, but it is advisable to gently guide conversation toward a counting of blessings now and then, to share something of a positive nature. Genuine caring that resulted in time-consuming creativity by Eileen's friend was sincerely appreciated and remembered.

Many of the widow's sensations are negative. She knows a traumatic sense of loss; she feels rejected, neglected, and inept. A variety of argumentative comments slip out. Don't feel overwhelmed by her negatives; they are only temporary and are a part of her necessary verbal therapy. It will pass, perhaps more slowly than you expect. Don't think you must offset all her negative remarks with positive ones. She will heal in time and needs someone who cares enough to sit quietly with her.

Being a good listener requires few words. It consists mostly of love, interest, and time. Every widow needs to talk over her troubles many times. It is also good therapy for her to relive the scene surrounding the death of her husband until she can finally release it permanently.

Encouraging her to relate the death story and

listening to it may seem morbid; but until she tells it many times during the weeks and months after her husband's death, it occupies a mammoth amount of her thinking. All else is of little importance in her mind, and she must talk about it or be silent, for she can concentrate on little else.

One possible breakthrough may be her children. She knows they share her loss and her feeling that nothing else has real value compared to the worth of their daddy.

Sheila, widowed only two weeks, said to me, "If I didn't have my daughter I wouldn't even get out of bed. It's just not worth it."

This is a time, too, when material objects lose worth and spiritual teachings are more readily accepted. The widow is interested not only in strength to get through each day but also in eternal life because of her late husband's encounter with eternity. Our Lord fulfills *all* our needs, temporal and eternal.

My God shall supply all your need according to his riches in glory by Christ Jesus (Phil. 4:19).

God is able to make all grace abound toward you; that ye, always having all sufficiency in all things, may abound to every good work (2 Cor. 9:8).

They that wait upon the Lord shall renew their strength; they shall mount up with wings as eagles; they shall run, and not be weary; and they shall walk, and not faint (Isa. 40:31).

This is the record, that God hath given to us eternal life, and this life is in his Son. He that hath the Son hath life; and he that hath not the Son of God hath not life. These things have I written unto you that believe on the name of the Son of God; that ye may know that ye have eternal life, and that ye may believe on the name of the Son of God. And this is the confidence that we have in him, that, if we ask any thing according to his will, he heareth us: and if we know that he hear us, whatsoever we ask, we know that we have the petitions that we desired of him (1 John 5:11–15).

Hearing and studying God's Word during my first year of widowhood led to a deeper understanding of His promises and changed the direction of my life from social service to service focused on Him. I valued His assurance above everything, but I appreciated human help more than I could express.

The following two incidents further illustrate effective positive actions and were shared by widows in their fifties.

"Henry just fell over dead on the kitchen floor and was gone. When the rescue squad was arriving, my daughter and her husband came, too. I really appreciated them, because they never left me by myself. Even after the funeral they came over and prepared supper here and ate with me each evening for weeks. I protested, saying I could be by myself, but they insisted. My grandsons, ages four and five, stayed all night with me for a month."

"It's good to have company," I agreed.

"Now here it is, six months later. I've had a lot of

27

quiet time to myself and am having a real problem trying to make myself get involved in anything again."

"I was grateful for the food people brought in," said another widow. "I was comforted by people telling me they loved me and were praying for me... I'm particularly enjoying one day each week. That's because a couple comes over and spends the day with me. We are labeling all the slides we took when my husband and I traveled with them to Israel last year. It's almost like taking the trip all over again. It's good to have someone to work with... I also appreciate it when people tell me how much they thought of my husband or mention some way he helped them."

There are six million widows in the United States. Only seven out of every hundred will remarry.

Widows need help, but unless we have experienced loss it is impossible to understand how the death of a loved one affects a person.

Can we provide answers to particular problems now facing the widow?

How can we find real peace of mind when we're too often afraid of our own emotions?

Have we an experience similar to the one the widow has just been through, or is facing, that will help us empathize?

The incidents in this chapter are not at all unusual. If you have been through widowhood, you know what each widow means by her words. If you have shared with a member of your family or a close friend who is familiar with the feelings involved in the death of a husband, you know the depth of emotion in each of the previous scenes.

Throughout this book we are going to talk about how widows usually react. This information will lead to understanding, not only for widows but more importantly for people who wish to help them.

We will talk about why each of us perceives death differently; how a self-help discussion group can be organized and maintained; what "normal" grief is; and how to inform the widow of her partner's death.

Then we are going to deal with some of the words and actions you can use to support widows. We will deal with how our presence comforts a widow and how to help her make decisions. We'll deal with mundane matters, such as the best kind of container to use when taking food to a bereaved person, or how to choose a card that really comforts. And we'll handle more complicated actions such as assisting with the children involved, helping the widow to find something to look forward to, and easing her adjustment. We will also talk about some things supportive people will avoid saying and doing.

In the next several chapters, then, we will discuss generally and specifically how people relate to death. We will deal with some practical suggestions for ministering to widows—things anyone can do to help. Finally, we will talk about ways to change how the world around us speaks to the issue of widowhood. Maybe we can make it easier for you, your daughter, or your grandaughter.

> *"When you are in the dark, listen, and
> God will give you a very precious
> message for someone else when you get
> into the light."*
> —Oswald Chambers

2

How Do You Perceive Death?

What we hear other people say and what we see
them do when death separates them from a loved
one affects the way we, ourselves, deal with death.
Looking back over the years, I see that I was introduced to the idea of death early but that I paid little
attention.

It is common to believe early in life that death
can't happen to us. In our twenties and thirties we
may think we are too young to be concerned just
yet. Gradually, we gain a deeper understanding of
life and death and accept both.

One of my earliest memories involved a widow.
She was our baby-sitter, Mrs. Toews. I recall her
setting me on our kitchen table, which was covered
by a red-and-white checkered oilcloth. She left me
there and went to get my father, who was teaching
next door. She wanted him to put a bandage on my

cheek, where I had cut it on a toy. I remember asking my father that evening, "Where is Mrs. Toews' husband?"

"Her husband died. Mrs. Toews is a widow and lives alone except for her son. She takes care of you and Joan while your mother and I teach, but she is also our school custodian," he said.

I can still see Mrs. Toews in my mind, tossing oiled sawdust on our school's old wooden floors each evening and then sweeping the halls and classrooms with a long-handled brush broom.

I don't remember her as a sad widow, even though she worked at two jobs and cared for a crippled son. I knew she had a monumental faith in God. She sang old hymns throughout the day. Trusting in Him and keeping busy helped her.

My second experience with death was closer. It came after my father accepted a position as superintendent of schools at a new location. We moved, and our new neighbors, the school custodian and his wife, became substitute grandparents for me. Since both of my parents corrected papers after school, I was free to visit Clara and Mage Prather often. I loved Clara. She was petite, like the dolls in her colorful collection. She told me that Mage could blow pipe smoke at a wart on my hand and make it go away. He did blow and it did go!

When I was eleven years old Mr. Prather died, and I attended my first funeral service. I hadn't really seen anyone grief-stricken before. I heard loud wails as that small widow followed the rest of us past the casket. As I looked back over my shoulder she appeared tiny, helpless, and terribly alone.

Death seemed very unfair and frightening to me then.

My next experience with death and a widow (for they seemed to belong together by now) was less than five years later. One of my favorite teachers, in addition to his teaching, farmed the land across the road from our house. I sometimes drove a tractor for him and cultivated corn during my early teen years when all our able young men had left for World War II. I knew his family well.

"Have you heard about Page?" a friend asked me one day. She had tears in her eyes.

"No, what happened?" My heart was thumping in my throat.

"He died in the field near his tractor." We later learned he'd had a brain hemorrhage. His widow was left with several small children.

After this third experience I began to have the feeling that married women couldn't count on having a mate for the rest of their lives.

So, as a senior in high school I listened when my father wisely suggested a teaching career for me. "It provides a fine schedule for widows with children," he counseled.

I began college. My childhood sweetheart Charlie and I were married the following June. That very summer my favorite uncle died. It was a pointed reminder, or so it seemed to me: Wise widows could teach school. My widowed aunt did, providing for herself and two daughters. I resolved anew that I would become an instructor.

As our children arrived and even after I began teaching to help my husband through college a second time, some inner voice seemed to repeat, *Daddy is right!* You could be widowed, so spend all the time with Charlie you can, and don't turn down invitations to share classes, trips, fun, and work with him.

I followed the guidance of those inner promptings, and I never had to feel guilty after Charlie's death. I shared every possible moment with him, even overcoming my fear of flying.

Since my husband's death I have talked to hundreds of widows; most feel unnecessary guilt about one thing or another. Long before statistics indicated that three out of four married American women face fourteen to eighteen years of widowhood, I began to contact other widows to ask and to answer questions.

The youngest widow I know is twenty-one and is adjusting well. The oldest is eighty-eight and is not quite certain why God leaves her alive.

The older widow admits bingo is the highlight of her week. She is delighted when she wins a small gift as a prize. She is confined to a large nursing home in an ancient building. Many of the people are hardly able to be active. Some can't see well enough to pass the time reading large-print books as she does; nearly all are lonely. Most are widows who need help in adjusting to a new way of life. A few are happy; many are bored and sad.

There will be as many reactions to life, to widowhood, and to our own impending death as there are individuals living and thinking about it. Age, independence, education, personality, and faith are a few of the many factors that make each of us react as we do.

Our heritage, environments, and experiences differ. We watch a variety of reactions to death around us. We read (or don't read!) different articles, stories, or books that affect us.

As a new widow I received invaluable, constant support from the Christian couple I mentioned in my introduction. They helped me move from disbelief in myself to confidence concerning my ability to assume, with the help of the Lord Jesus, my new role. My next step was to educate myself further regarding adjustment to widowhood, so as to prepare myself to share vital information with other widows.

Opportunities to counsel and console other widows, on a one-to-one basis, began to come my way several months after I was widowed. Then one day five years later, I received a request to visit three Omaha women who had recently lost their husbands in a Chicago airplane crash.

After meeting these women and sharing their grief, both they and the others I had been visiting with began to meet as a group. We discussed how we could reach out to other widows. Our self-help group grew out of this desire.

"Solitaires" is the name we selected for our group. To us it means set alone (like a diamond in a ring), valued and beautiful, reflecting God's light.

Some of our verbal comments are in this book, along with some written answers from questionnaires shared with widows across America. We trust they will help you understand why widows sometimes can't get out of bed to face another day, why some of us cry so long, or how one small upsetting occurrence can throw us totally off balance. We beg you to understand simple things like how a constricted throat makes it impossible to swallow anything but Jello! Most of all, we hope we can offer the insight you need to be a special friend to the widows you know.

3

Solitaires

Some of you may wonder why a book for those who want to "visit widows in their affliction" would include a chapter on how to begin a *self*-help group. After all, doesn't the term "self-help" imply that those with a particular problem work out solutions together, without outside assistance?

A self-help group *is* for those who are experiencing similar problems. However, the impetus for starting such a group does not have to come from someone who is in the problem situation himself. If you are concerned about the needs of widows (which you must be since you are reading this book), then perhaps you are the one to help the widows you know establish a self-help group. We recommend, however, that widows be the officers and take some leadership responsibility as soon as possible.

The following suggestions are born out of the experience of those who first established Solitaires—a group designed specifically to help widows.

First, we listed the time and place for a widows' discussion group in the local newspaper, and then we met in one home for three consecutive Thursday nights to await the results. In attendance were four, eight, and then fifteen women. We decided to meet once a month.

During those first three meetings, we found a rapport among ourselves that none of us had found elsewhere. We were finally free to ask questions we had been reluctant to ask relatives, and we found we could release emotions we had long repressed—even with our closest friends.

We discussed how a lack of preparation for facing death affected us. We talked about actions that helped us and words we wished people would have used to console us. We repeated the disturbing remarks, advice, and suggestions that penetrated our deep shock and sounded like crashing cymbals when our nerves demanded a soft touch. We learned that our hallucinations are normal and that a few of us find sexual release in dreams.

"Be gentle with yourself," we began to advise one another.

One twice-widowed lady insisted that those who will adjust best to life in all areas are busy, independent, positive-thinking women who feel challenged rather than defeated by problems. We knew it could take years of preparation to fulfill her one-sentence requirement, but we decided to begin.

Once organized, we accepted an offer from Rev.

Keith Cook and his congregation to use their church free of charge. The mission committee of the Presbyterian Church of the Master gives us economic and prayer support. (Not much money is needed, however.)

We use the money to print letters explaining who we are and what our purpose is and for mailing meeting notices to those interested enough to inquire.

We have learned to add a couple of names and telephone numbers to *all* our correspondence. Then anyone who has a question or wishes to have a friend or relative invited can call us.

Of course, not all groups will be able to find a rent-free meeting place, but there are other options. Some banks have meeting rooms that they allow the public to rent. If you charge each widow a small fee at every meeting you can collect enough money to match such expenses, depending on the population in your town and the attendance at your meetings.

We use our local Christian radio station and the club news section in the newspaper to announce the date and agenda of the monthly meeting. We are grateful for the publicity given free to service organizations. Most radio stations and newspapers will make announcements if information is neatly typed on a postcard or a half sheet of paper and mailed ten days in advance of the regular meeting. A local television host asked members of our group to explain our purpose to the community. This was an excellent opportunity for us to encourage other widows to join us and to make others aware of our needs.

At most meetings we have a speaker who is

trained and able to give guidelines in areas that
concern widows. We have had ministers, doctors,
psychotherapists, lawyers, and bankers. You will
think of others. We schedule our speakers two or
three months in advance. They are busy people
who are willing to donate their time, which we are
careful to acknowledge by a thank-you note. An
honorarium of five or ten dollars may be considered, but that will require monthly dues or a regular
contribution by those attending. Widows, generally, are counting pennies.

Our speakers are allowed about thirty minutes. A
question-and-answer period follows. We especially
enjoy splitting up into small groups for discussion
during our meetings. Our time together is limited
(usually around two hours), but deep and meaning-
ful sharing takes place throughout the evening. We
meet in the evening because most widows work
regular daytime hours.

Coffee and cookies are served. Money put into a
small box when obtaining refreshments is on a vol-
untary basis and is sometimes spent on get-well
cards and postage stamps.

Our names and telephone numbers are shared
only with one another. We duplicate lists so we can
get better acquainted, even though we may be from
opposite sides of town.

Since our group has grown larger we have
elected hostesses and officers who have loosely
established duties. Past officers frequently continue to attend as advisors.

Our expanded ministry has included city-wide,
well-publicized seminars held five Tuesday nights

in a row featuring top speakers and resulting in response by fifty widows at a time. We charge a dollar per person each evening during seminars for coffee and cookie expenses. With any remaining money we purchase books to give away.

A few widows are hesitant about coming at first. They may clip out notices from the paper, put them away for safekeeping, and then call months later when they feel more capable of coping.

We are beginning to mail letters that explain who we are, state our purpose, give our monthly meeting time and place, and welcome the widow to call or come and meet with us. Below is a sample letter:

Dear Mrs._____ ,

Do you have a question you'd like to ask another widow? We have an informal discussion group in Omaha whose purpose is to share experiences, answer questions, and help widows in adjusting. We are all ages, Christian in focus but interdenominational, and represent a wide variety of churches. We have no actual membership list or dues, but those who want to may donate a quarter each meeting to help defray the cost of coffee, cookies, printing, and postage.

We meet at Presbyterian Church of the Master the first Tuesday night of each month, at 7:30 p.m. (Presbyterian Church of the Master is a block south and a half block east of the 108th and Maple corner, just west of Interstate 680.)

We recommend two books: GOOD GRIEF by Granger Westberg, and TOP OF THE VALLEY by Mary Brite, either of which can be purchased at local Christian bookstores, and each of which costs only $1.25.

We frequently have a speaker at our meeting who covers an area regarding our adjustment, and we also discuss our problems in small groups some time during the evening. Do stop in and get acquainted. Our meeting area is safe for you at night.

QUESTIONS?   Call: Jane Doe 000-0000 or _____ _____ 000-0000.

May God comfort you,

_____ , Advisor
Solitaires

We sometimes mail these letters to widows whose relatives have called us, or even to those listed in the daily obituary column as being "left" by Mr. John Doe, at a certain address, whose funeral is today or tomorrow. We hold these for a couple of weeks before mailing them to avoid some of the confusion surrounding the widow during her first days of shock.

Some women resent being put into the category of "widow." We have been reprimanded for addressing them as Mary Doe instead of Mrs. John Doe, so be cautious concerning etiquette. Many women want their husband's name used for a while, even if they usually used "Mary" before the death.

We also present a variety of helpful books to first-timers at our monthly meetings, and we try immediately to communicate to new widows how helpful books can be.

Our Solitaires group meets the needs of most who visit. We try to make everyone feel at home. Once in a while someone who is widowed and sharing with the group feels left out because of a particular differing circumstance or personality. One evening we had been speaking for several minutes concerning the adjustment involved for our children—only to realize that some widows present had no children and were feeling especially lonely during those moments.

A few refuse to return, not wishing to be "stuck" with widows. Some don't want to be where there are no men. Once in a while one is upset at having been reminded openly of her husband's death. She isn't ready to think about it (face it or admit it), so she prefers not to share with us at all yet. She may return later.

During our meetings many of these lonely women find others who have similar interests. They may meet for meals, to attend the community playhouse, go shopping, play golf or tennis, or swap recipes. A few have even vacationed together, some with their two sets of children, as friendships grow.

If a widow is having a tearful time during our monthly meeting, others rally around to empathize. We encourage her and assure her it gets easier as time goes along. Anyone allowing the group to know she is very depressed will certainly receive some telephone calls of cheer during the following days and weeks. We care.

It has taken about three years for news to spread by word of mouth that we are here, organized, meeting monthly, and willing to contact widows. Notifying other services or social agencies about our group quickens this process. We are now receiving references from concerned relatives seeking help for loved ones in grief, or telephone calls asking for further information. Widows adjust and move past a point of needing us, so we are always ready to draw in new members.

A survey in Omaha shows that less than six churches (out of hundreds) actually have widow-, single-, or divorcée-oriented programs. We are beginning, however. So can you.

If we want to be obedient to God and if we read the Scripture verse quoted at the beginning of this chapter, we will see as we seek to understand its deeper meaning that we are commanded to help widows and their children.

If women or couples visit widows, rather than men alone helping them, it eliminates potential problems in relationships.

The chairman of a widows' group can be more effective in helping others if she has been widowed a couple of years and is safely through her own worst crisis periods. The first few times I tried to help I ended up crying and needing comfort myself when I arrived home after the meetings.

It helps if two or three agree to share the responsibility of a new group, but one person can do it all and obtain help after it is well organized. I did. If the leaders are well-adjusted and have outgoing personalities, the group will be able to offer help to those attending more quickly.

We found it helpful to limit regular attendance to widows only. Smaller towns might want to combine groups and include divorced women. Many of the problems are very much related—accepting loss, feeling out of place, needing careers, helping children adjust.

Our group is Christian in focus, but interdenominational. Helping each widow to know Jesus as Lord and Savior is one of our goals. God blesses our group. We strive to provide inspiration at each meeting, but we cover practical ideas for adjustment, too. We don't want to "be so heavenly minded that we are no earthly good."

We believe a widow needs to learn that God loves her just as she is and wants to help her. Then she may call on Him when the night is long and lonely, when friends and relatives are away, or when she prefers not to bother anyone else.

A friend of mine who has been through training for Christian counseling shared with me that the lower the widow's self-acceptance, the greater the depression and trauma will be. (I see this as I work with widows.) Severe emotional problems may show up as you listen to and observe widows. A mind under too much pressure from emotional trauma sets up self-protective defenses called neuroses. Later, if unchecked, these defenses become psychoses.

Some symptoms of these defenses are anxiety, guilt, fear, and anger. We all have these normal symptoms, but when the anxiety is extreme or lasts too long, the widow has a problem.

A widow may use these defenses to adapt reality by perceiving only what she wants to perceive and by ignoring the threatening parts. Thus reality is repressed.

More serious signs of defense are denial, isola-
tion, rationalism, repression, and regression. These
lead to compensation and fantasy. When approaching psychosis the signs are avoidance and with-
drawal.

The key to helping anyone is not to try to change
them. That is God's business. We need to accept
widows and encourage them to know they are acceptable to us and to God just as they are. Their
personalities will change automatically as they are
able to know how much God loves them. As we
lovingly encourage them in their self-worth, with
gentle nudges toward pursuing new responsibilities and interests when they are able, the healing will progress normally.

It is ultimately important for people to have direction and purpose for living! We must have a
purpose—not a program (or the "when" and "how"
in *all detail,* which may cause nervous break-
downs). The troubled mind of a grieving widow is
already overloaded; she doesn't need more added
to it. She needs to be given some hope for going on,
to know God still has a plan for her life, perhaps
with some changes in direction.

If you pray for guidance with sensitivity as to
what she is ready for, you will help her to be able to
heal and grow. Most Christian people and many
pastors feel Scripture and admonishment will take
care of all the problems a Christian has. But if a
widow is not emotionally and spiritually mature,
her mind cannot hear or understand enough to receive your advice because it is already overloaded
with her own trauma. As self-acceptance grows, the

ability to receive spiritual teaching and Scripture will come. Love her and give her all the time she needs to grow.*

As we work with widows, we find others who are seeking help for themselves or friends. Several Solitaires have been asked such questions as:

"Where is a group for parents who have lost a child?" and "Are grandparents allowed in that group?"

"Where can I find friends? I'm new in town—single, female, thirty, and tired of married men and bars!"

"Where is a Christian group for a divorced mother?"

If you decide to organize a self-help group, be assured that you don't have to be academically prepared. Experience and maturity are worth a priceless amount. A nationally known Omaha psychiatrist, Dr. Beverley Mead, praised our Solitaires group and told us, "The best understanding, help, and leadership come from those who have been through the agony of loss and have found hope and life again. Solitaires has enough structure to provide order and security but still keeps vital and flexible. Don't try to make the group like formal group therapy."

We are beginning to help organize other groups for widows nearby. Three of us have spoken at universities, at a seminar for doctors, and to groups who are interested in helping the elderly.

After two of us had driven several hours to speak

---

*The preceding paragraphs are adapted from the teaching of Jeanette Collins, Bible study teacher and Christian counselor.

to priests and bishops of the Episcopal churches in South Dakota, we had an experience that made years of effort worthwhile. They all expressed an affirmative "AMEN" after our closing prayer. The deliciously warm feeling returns when I write of it here.

We hope that widows who have had time to adjust will form a small committee, present this idea to their pastors, receive backing from their church lay leaders, and begin to help in their own locations. A qualified person who is not a widow can take the lead, too. It's a responsibility, but it's rewarding!

*"If we understand and tolerate the periods of
pain as they come, we free ourselves to
move ahead."*
—Author

4

What is Normal?

Each working night seems to grow darker and
longer, Wauneta thought, not knowing the length
and depth of darkness this particular night would
bring. Six months pregnant, she found her nursing
uniform overly snug as she attempted to button it.

"Let's put on your coat and go see Grandmother,"
she said as she finished stuffing two-year-old
Tommy into his pajamas.

"I wish you'd learn to talk," she said, and then
erased threatening thoughts from her mind regarding his lack of progress in learning to speak.

Moments later she handed the husky child to his
grandmother. Tommy's large brown eyes, framed
with long lashes like his daddy's, looked tired.

"Robert will pick him up on the way home from
work as usual in a couple of hours. Thanks, Mom.
See you tomorrow," Wauneta called over her
shoulder as she left for night duty as an LPN.

Wauneta was alarmed when she received a telephone call at 2:00 A.M. at the hospital. Dreadful thoughts tumbled over one another as she listened.

"Your husband has a serious injury from an automobile accident. Please come to the emergency room at Methodist."

Wauneta told the head nurse she had to leave and rushed across town to the hospital. When she saw Robert, she knew immediately that he was dead.

"It's all right. You aren't to blame," she heard herself saying through her shock, consoling the shaken young chaplain as he tried to tell her about the drunken driver who had crashed into Robert's car. A coldness crept over her body.

Later, Wauneta couldn't properly explain to Tommy why his father wasn't there for their regular romping time each afternoon. Tommy withdrew further into a world of his own. Tina, born three months later, never knew her family complete with a father's love.

We met Wauneta, even though she lived in a small town thirty miles away, because a mutual friend had heard of our visits with widows on a one-to-one basis, and asked us to come and talk with her. As a result, she came to our widow's self-help therapy group for our second organizational meeting. She assured us that she had absolutely no problems, had everything under control, and never would need any help—then promptly ran from the family room into the kitchen, put her head down on the table and cried uncontrollably.

"This is the first time I've truly been able to talk to anyone about my feelings," she said a few minutes later when she had been held and comforted.

She had no need to conceal her mental agitation from our group. We had already seen through her disguise. We empathized with her. We had all groveled our way through undesirable unknowns.

Each of us, offering encouragement from our own experience, was able to contribute something in the valuable discussion that followed. Her self-doubts had been ours, and her struggle to adjust made those of us who had conquered similar problems grateful that we were a few steps ahead and able to aid someone else.

Wauneta's denial, followed by her honesty, proved beneficial to all. An openness grew within the group that has never left.

Several frustrating years have passed. Wauneta has experienced shock, loneliness, and grief. Tommy refused to begin talking for another eighteen months after Robert's death. He was diagnosed as autistic. The special care and understanding Tommy requires has added to Wauneta's burden physically and mentally. Extra patience has been needed when it has been hard to find strength to continue living at all. Wauneta has faced a serious lack of funds needed to obtain expensive professional help for Tommy. Even finding understanding baby-sitters for him has been hard, restricting her activities.

I once visited her in answer to a hysterical midnight telephone call. Tommy had set the house on fire! She had controlled the blaze but had burned her hands and ruined a coat in smothering it, and she needed assurance.

No one has fully understood or shared her burden. Three church congregations have missed an opportunity. Wauneta is searching and screaming for help—even a small portion.

Tommy is beginning to function more normally and is about to be accepted into a regular classroom situation. Tina is well adjusted and understands Tommy in a special way, but Wauneta has tough years ahead of her.

She knows God loves her and is often able to express her gratitude for blessings. She has overcome some hectic times with a marvelous sense of humor.

Because of her particular situation, Wauneta has been more concerned than most widows about what is "normal."

"Is it normal to feel guilty?"

"Should I be bitter?"

"Is it wrong to be mad at God?"

All of us are concerned with being right-minded, so it helps to know there are rational and real stages of grief. To know what milestones are along the road and how they appear is to travel the road less fearfully. Then when we recognize an emotion in ourselves or someone we are trying to help we can say, "Oh, yes, I remember it is normal to feel this way!" If we understand and tolerate the periods of pain as they come, we free ourselves to move ahead.

A mother who has lost a child or a man who is denied a job promotion after thirty years of work will go through the same phases as the widow, although perhaps on a different level of intensity.

The mother, the man, and the widow are forced to face and work through grief if each wishes to remain sane. To stay in one of the stages for years is to be diagnosed as neurotic. Each person is educated and experienced in his own individual way, so each will proceed at his own pace—perhaps inverting the order, staying in one stage for a longer or shorter length of time than someone else, or even skipping one transition entirely. The terminally ill person works through similar stages.

Headings for the following paragraphs are shortened chapter titles from *Good Grief* by Granger Westberg,[1] which describes the steps of progress through grief. We recommend this reasonably priced, well-written book to each new widow we meet and frequently give them away at our meetings.

This small book helped me six months after my husband died, and my only frustration then was not having found it sooner.

Below are Westberg's stages. The explanations and examples that follow are from my own experiences with widows. We believe these emotions are acceptable and will be experienced.

Shock

One element of shock might be described as the "stun reaction," says Dr. Mead (the psychiatrist introduced in Chapter 3). This is the frozen or blunted emotional response often observed initially and sometimes misinterpreted by observers as "she doesn't care," simply because there isn't a sudden outburst of emotional storm.

Some sentences heard during our widows' self-help discussion groups regarding early days of widowhood were:

"I was in a trance."

"I didn't know what I was saying."

"I couldn't believe it."

"I just functioned mechanically."

"I only heard part of what he said."

"It just didn't register."

"I couldn't remember my best friend's name."

Each of these widows felt a temporary, natural escape, because of the way God created us. Although this stage allows us to face reality a small bit at a time, it also seems to short-circuit some of our other thought processes. We seem to function from habit, mechanically. We may not know what we are doing, where we put things, what we just said, what day it is, or how long it has been since the funeral. Our minds are on our dead husbands instead of today's activities.

Emotion

We cry. For various reasons we sometimes postpone it. I believe it is safe to say we will not get over the pain and grief until we have spent much time crying. Some widows begin to allow themselves to feel and think more freely from this point forward. It hurts, but then healing can begin. How terribly hard this tears stage of grief is for the male in our society; "Don't cry; you're a man!"

Various memories, sights, events, words, or music may trigger tears.

"I heard our song and tears flooded my face," Eva said.

"I chased a man down the street for a block before he turned his head and I could see his profile. I cried when I recalled that Bob was dead. For a moment I thought it was him," Fran explained.

We need not subscribe to Zeno's Stoic Greek philosophy of 308 B.C., which states that since all happenings are the result of divine will we should calmly accept them and be free from passion, grief, or joy.[2] I also believe the divine will is involved, but I appreciate being allowed to express myself. (Too many Christians are afraid to exhibit any of these three.) If I couldn't, I'd be like an armored knight left on the field of battle to be discovered years later, firm on the outside but disintegrated inside.

Our Lord denied Zeno's Stoicism when He cried at the death of Lazarus. Modern psychologists and counselors know that to repress grief is to bring on mental illness and instability.

I like C. S. Lovett's comment as he explains a deeper meaning underlying John 11:35: "God cries. He is not merely a spectator to human heartache, but a participator. 'Jesus wept'. . . . Tears then are not a defect, but perfectly in order for God and man. Our Savior is far more attractive as a weeping, loving Lord, than as an unfeeling, unconcerned stoic. He felt Mary's pain—even as He feels ours!"[3]

The widow should be allowed tears. Friends and relatives should realize they will be accepted as caring if they join her.

It won't always be this way. Praise the Lord there's a day coming when none of His children will cry! "And God shall wipe away all tears from their eyes; and there shall be no more death, neither sorrow, nor crying, neither shall there be any more pain: for the former things are passed away" (Rev. 21:4).

Depression and Loneliness

These are feelings the widow has experienced before during her life, but they dive deeper now. It makes no difference how many people are around her; she still feels isolated. The one she loved most is gone and all the world seems empty to her.

"I had friends all around me in the room but I felt as if they were walled off from me," Grace told us.

"They were all couples and I was definitely out of place," Geneva said.

It's a very normal feeling.

Physical Depression

A new widow may experience a hesitancy in her speech. Talking slowly like a record dragging along on the wrong speed is normal. So is talking faster than usual.

Don't be surprised if the widow needs to have information or questions repeated. It's a sign of shock.

Jeanette Collins, now a Christian counselor, was widowed very young and experienced a memory and concentration problem:

> After being widowed at the age of twenty-five, I became very discouraged with a chronic loss of concentration and memory. I tried two jobs the

first year, but my mind didn't function well enough to keep them. When my boss gave me instructions, I tried desperately to listen; but what little I comprehended would leave me in a few minutes.

I even accompanied my parents and sister on two or three trips in the months that followed, but later I could remember nothing about them. Gradually my mental faculties improved, but my memory never has been the same after that.

In recent years I've found some answers to this problem, common to most widows in varying degrees. Through counseling training I learned that the mind cannot function adequately under emotional stress or while in shock and trauma. The mind can only handle a certain amount of information. When shock is present, confusion causes the brain to overload and partially short-circuit. This is nature's way of giving the mind a temporary rest.

It explains why people in grief weep for short periods at a time. Then they can laugh and participate socially somewhat again—almost feeling the tragedy isn't real after all. Most widows experience these phases intermittently for some time.

Many widows catch colds or become ill and stay in bed for days. *Bereaved persons need to eat and rest properly, both of which are hard to do at this time.* Neglecting these vital needs can add to the possibility of physical illness.

Rest is something relatives try to guarantee as they protect widows from too much pressure (and sometimes visitors) during the first weeks of widowhood.

"I didn't have enough energy to get up. Why bother? There wasn't anything worth getting out of bed to see or do," Hannah told me. She had no children, no job, and no nearby relatives.

Panic

A widow frequently worries about losing her mind. This points an accusing finger at our society, which refuses to face the fact of death. She may have unfounded fears about other aspects of her life, at times mentally building giant-sized financial problems even though she may be adequately cared for by insurance or a good job. Her whole world seems to be tipped and falling. Sometimes, however, these fears are well founded.

"I'm paying for the cemetery plots, the casket, and my college child's air ticket here and back. I've provided extra clothing for my younger ones for the funeral and I had to buy a black dress. I'll be broke." Joan's husband left no insurance.

"My friend had to borrow grocery money because they froze the bank account." (It happens in some states!)

When bills all arrive at once it is hard to remain calm and realize that money may balance out soon. For some widows it *won't* balance. The average widow lives on $6,000 a year.

Guilt

Most individuals feel some guilt about something they said or didn't say to a loved one. The

mature Christian asks God's forgiveness and forgives herself also. If she cannot forgive herself and
also allow herself to forget, her normal guilt may
turn into neurotic guilt.

"My husband wanted a son and I didn't want
more children. I only have girls," Janice confided
to me. It was eye-opening for this widow to realize
later that she could probably rear girls more easily
than boys with her past personal experience. She
overcame her guilt and allowed herself to feel gratitude for her girls.

"I wish I hadn't been too tired from working all
day to have sex sometimes," Jeannine said.

"I wish I had tried to make him happier. He was
good to me," said another widow.

"We had a terrible argument the week before he
died and it was my fault."

Guilt is not limited to widows. Children experience it too. My minister, Norman Hagley, tells of a
young man who visited with him frequently. "He
seemed to have something on his mind but was
reluctant to talk about it. The friendship grew over a
period of days and weeks. Eventually the conversation included discussion of a time earlier when the
young man's father had asked him to put up some
storm windows on the house. As might be expected,
the chore wasn't welcomed and the young man left
it undone and went off to a ball game. As might also
be expected, the father did the job himself. The
next day the father died of a heart attack. It's sad,
but the young man felt a deep sense of guilt for
seven years."

Mother or someone needs to carefully discuss
this particular aspect or stage of grief—guilt—with

each child, so no member of the family will continue to harbor guilt.

We can stand with our feet firmly supported by God's Word when we urge others to release guilt feelings. He made us only a little lower than the angels; He loved us enough to send His Son to save us from sin; He forgives us all our sins and separates them from us as far as the east is from the west.* With God the Father as our Source, can we do less than love and forgive ourselves?

Hostility and Resentment

A widow usually seeks someone to blame. She may blame *anyone* connected to the situation in which her husband died. She may become bitter toward the physician, God, or even her lost partner. This is normal.

Sometimes resentment is directed *toward* the widow by grieving relatives who blame her for her husband's death. This is especially hard on the widow, who needs her loved ones most at this time.

Maybe you understand anger and bitterness to be quite different from hostility and resentment. We are usually surprised to discover anger in ourselves and ashamed to admit it. Bereaved people, especially, may think something is wrong with them if they feel anger toward someone who has just died. To the inexperienced that may seem monstrous; we recognize and accept guilt more readily than anger.

"I hate you for leaving me with these children to rear by myself," one widow shouted at her dead and

---

*See Heb. 2:7; John 3:16; Ps. 103:3; Ps. 103:12.

buried husband. She resented being burdened with the total responsibility for nine youngsters.

Relatives from the husband's side of the family need to be understanding of an attitude such as this, which is very normal.

The widow may unthinkingly forget that her mother-in-law has suffered a great loss, too. Even in remembering, she may assume her loss to be greater and mentally downgrade her mother-in-law's loss.

Inability to Face Usual Activities

If you and I learn to accept and talk about death, the widow won't have to carry her grief around inside herself; she will be able to share thoughts and feelings more easily and will want to be with us earlier in her adjustment. Being with people who deny death increases a widow's feeling of uneasiness about being normal. She has to accept death *as a fact* each new day, even when we refuse to accept it.

"They never mention him. They even act like he never existed. I can't talk to them because he is *all* I think of and want to talk about," Jane said between sobs. She was talking about her lifelong friends.

Hope

Sometimes hope is evidenced when the widow forgets herself and changes her direction enough to help someone else.

"I was able to help someone I met at the luncheon today. She was asking the same questions

I asked two years ago. Her children are not the same age as mine, but we have much in common," Helen said excitedly. The idea of being able to help someone else lifted her morale considerably.

A New and Different Reality

The widow finally returns to a more effective life, although she will definitely be a different person because of her experience, probably a stronger, deeper, more capable person. She would cherish such a compliment if you carefully expressed it to her when you feel she has progressed to this final stage. Remember, she definitely needs encouragement all along the way.

"What determines the amount of time it takes a widow to adjust?" I asked my friend who has been widowed twice and has adjusted well both times.

"The type of individual each widow is, the amount of emotion she allows herself to show, the profession she follows, and the level of society she lives within are qualities that may affect the way a woman adapts to widowhood," she replied. "She will be affected by her total background, the number of children she has and their ages, her own health, interests, and finances.

"She may be even more individualistic in the way she adjusts, depending on how much love she felt for her husband, whether she knew in advance he was going to die, and certainly by her philosophy of life and acceptance of reality," she continued.

I waited quietly for her to consider my question a bit longer.

"Those who work through the stages of grief most satisfactorily probably number among their attributes a past that has been used successfully to develop individuality and a personality that doesn't live constantly within the shadow of a husband. Perhaps she has learned something about the business of the family, the care of an automobile, and several other things outside her own kitchen and cleaning closet. She has learned to think for herself about most large and small decisions that need to be made daily within the framework of any marriage—long before the day she is widowed."

Widows without children, although they identify well with other widows, carry an extra burden of loneliness. They may need more activities to fill their time. One widow who didn't have children began to worry about whether her husband had actually loved her or not, since she had no child to show for her years of marriage. She was told by another in our group, "The fact that you were married to him proved that he loved you even if you didn't have children."

Widows can help one another. You can learn to be effective in supporting them, too.

[1]Granger E. Westberg, *Good Grief* (Philadelphia: Fortress, 1971).

[2]Webster's *New World Dictionary* (Cleveland: The World Publishing Co., 1966).

[3]C. S. Lovett, *Lovett's Lights on John* (Baldwin Park, Ca.: Personal Christianity, 1969), p. 196.

"A willing helper does not wait to be called."
—Danish proverb

5

Informing and Comforting the Widow

After visiting with widows for some time we found that many had bitter complaints against medical personnel who knew in advance that their husbands were probably not going to live but were uneasy about how such news would be accepted and so avoided it altogether.

Elisabeth Kubler-Ross explains why this is done and gives examples in her book *On Death and Dying*.[1] Basically, she says, such actions have their foundation in our society's lack of open communication regarding death.

We have discussed with widows the methods used to inform them of their husbands' deaths. Sometimes the widow has to guess what the one notifying her is trying to say.

"People should have more straightforward honesty," Corinne said. "Without being hard or cruel, tell the truth. Leave out half-baked answers. They shouldn't push the job of telling you onto someone else or shirk what they should say."

There are situations where the truth is not known by medical personnel regarding the possibility of death, but giving *false* hope will probably be resented later.

"My doctor assured me my husband was improving. Three days later he was dead," Carol bitterly told me. Her husband was a fireman who had inhaled too much smoke.

Many widows want more understanding by those who tell them of their husband's death. Often notification of death is done crudely, with an attitude of *anything to get it over with in a hurry*.

"Are you Mrs. Jones?"

"Yes."

"I'm from the sheriff's department. Your husband has just been killed in an automobile accident."

Please! If you are a person notifying a widow:

1. Take time to be sure that a friend or loved one is with her now and will stay immediately following such news.
2. Be certain children are not standing nearby to overhear. They should be told with loving arms around them.
3. Express at least one warning phrase, such as, "I'm sorry to be bringing bad news to you," or "Your husband was involved in an accident." It cushions or prepares her enough to brace herself for the shock.

"You feel like being left alone," Geri said. "Later

you realize it was better not to have been left entirely alone, even if the one person you would have
wanted to be with you couldn't be there." She was
twenty-three and had no children. She and her
husband had a vicious argument just before he left
the house, and she felt guilty because he was killed
in a one-car accident minutes later.

A widow will not be spared shock or grief no
matter what is said, but she may never forget what
was said and *how* it was said, so think carefully
before speaking.

Dr. Mead says that in talking to medical students
about breaking bad news to family members, he
usually includes these simple admonitions: "Tell
him or her alone, sitting down, with tissues handy.
Stay with him or her while feelings are expressed.
Before leaving, ask who else needs to be told,
when, and by whom."

You may be one of those who hears the news next.
If so, remember that your presence, more than anything else, comforts the widow. However, it is also
wise for friends to assess the situation early after the
husband's death and decide if there are too many
people surrounding the widow. She may have too
many people ringing the doorbell. She may need
rest more than company.

Any widow is pleased with the presence and
attention of those she loves when her shock is less.
It might be helpful if a couple of friends or relatives
would agree to stay and the rest were urged to
return home immediately after the funeral. Friends
and relatives should return when the confusion
calms.

The reverse might also be true. Several close friends may need to take turns visiting with a lonely widow who has few concerned people around. Perhaps she is older and has children living a long distance away. She may need company immediately and regularly.

A friend shared the following experience with me.

"Two days after Dad's funeral an assistant director from the funeral home stopped by with the copies of the death certificate and returned a pair of socks in a small paper bag. He was a kind young man and sat and had a cup of coffee with my mother, who proceeded to pour out her feelings about the funeral. She talked about how it was handled, of feeling rushed through it, listing good things and constructive criticisms. My daughter and I were in the kitchen and could overhear the conversation. Finally my daughter asked, 'Who is he—the therapist they send out after the funeral?'

" 'I wish there were such a service,' I said, 'but you know, he's doing a pretty good job!' If you have someone who cares about you and *listens,* you won't *need* a therapist later."

One of the things churches could do is to have something like a Funeral Follow-up Committee, composed of caring persons whose specific task would be to maintain weekly contact with bereaved persons for a year or more.

Too often, by the time people are needed they have returned to their own responsibilities and the widow feels abandoned. A deep feeling of loneliness may last as long as eighteen months after the funeral.

Do come back later.

[1]Elisabeth Kubler-Ross, *On Death and Dying* (New York: Macmillan, 1969).

> *"Tomorrow has two handles: the handle of fear and the handle of faith. You can take hold of it by either handle."*
> —Author Unknown

6

decisions, Decisions,
DECISIONS!

The list of decisions begins with the day, time, and type of funeral. It continues through finding information to take to the Social Security office and lawyer, getting death certificates (usually ten at three dollars each), and proceeds through whether or not the widow shall move to something smaller because of home maintenance and lawn responsibilities.

The widow is ordinarily responsible for the choice of burial plots. I bought two in Colorado Springs by telephone from Kansas, sight unseen.

By the time Charlie's body was released in Kansas and we had driven home, relatives had been notified and had arrived from all parts of the United States. They were waiting for final decisions to be made regarding the services.

My living room sounded as if a bunch of bees had

swarmed in, and my strongest impulse was to run back to my bedroom and hide under the bed. I didn't want to see anyone or talk at all. I definitely did not want to make decisions. But I had to—there was no choice.

Choosing a casket was easy for me; Charlie loved to work with his hands and had done woodworking, so I chose one in a warm-colored wood. I was not pressured and I had relatives with me who were able to think clearly. They were wise in urging me not to overspend, using money that might be needed later for my children and their education.

Here is something most important: Someone needs to gently reassure every widow that she and her husband shared a love that will be neither enhanced nor diminished by the value of the casket she chooses. She also needs to be reminded that guilt about something she did or didn't do or say to her husband is a *normal reaction.* Such guilt will not be erased by an expensive box lined in his favorite color.

The widow may receive suggestions from a pastor concerning arrangements for the funeral service. In spite of humor poked at clergymen during the daily lives of many Americans, when death enters the picture other individuals and agencies are dismissed, and someone more informed regarding eternity is sought. A good pastor can conduct a good funeral. Don't feel as if you have to make decisions about the conduct of the service. (Don't make decisions you don't have to, and put off all that don't have to be made today. I appreciated being reminded, "You don't have to make *that* decision

72

today.") You may simply want to say to the pastor, "Please conduct a service that emphasizes hope and new life."

People commented on the uniqueness of the resurrection music at Charlie's funeral. Some said they had never heard it played or sung at a funeral. It was helpful to me.

I decided to take our young children to the funeral of their father. Any past funeral experience shared by my children and me would have been invaluable. We had none. I wish we had had; it could have prepared the groundwork for better understanding and communication between us.

I decided to talk about the tragedy. Thank the Lord for that decision! I was blessed by relatives and friends who sat and listened over and over again to my story of finding Charlie's crashed airplane. I didn't realize it until later, but my best therapy began the first time I told it all the way through.

I didn't cry for five months. I wasn't covering up; I just felt like a block of ice. I was certain that when I thawed out, I would melt away and there would be nothing left of me at all. At first I didn't feel enough to cry. I was just numb.

Then I decided I wouldn't cry because I thought my four children would think I was adjusting and accepting death better if they didn't see tears from me. Finally, when I thought it would be a relief to cry, I couldn't.

Denise, a very mature widow, told me of her somewhat similar situation regarding tears. "My

husband died of leukemia, and I thought I was
prepared for his death because I had a year to get
ready. But when the release came for him in death,
I found none for myself in life. By that time my
practiced patience and pretenses appeared nearly
natural. It was impossible for me to free my genuine
locked-in emotions. Loving relatives realized what
was happening to me. They provided the key by
prearranged conversation. My tears came. Then
healing could begin." She had wise relatives who
loved her very much and decided to do something
constructive.

Endless decisions regarding changes begin at
once: cleaning out the husband's desk, sorting or
packing or giving away his clothing, and maybe
even procedures for selling a business.

A widow should not make any major decisions
quickly or without unbiased advice," says Rev. J.
Keith Cook, pastor of Presbyterian Church of the
Master in Omaha. "Delay is good if it does not
linger into mere avoidance of reality. Don't decide
to sell the house or car until you need to make that
decision—no 'ought to' decisions.

"Regarding the disposal of the husband's clothes,
it is good to do that soon so the widow doesn't
decide to enshrine his closet and his dresser drawers, awaiting his return. The fact is, he died, and the
act of removing his things helps us cope with that
reality. At the same time there need not be a grand
sweep of *all* his things. Keep representative
mementos, such as his watch, his pen set, his
billfold—those things the widow, his children, and
grandchildren will enjoy as remembrances."

These are decisions and labors with a purpose. Share them with the widow if she will let you. If you have a good suggestion, verbalize it gently. Let her make all final decisions. She knows the overall situation best. There is a need to take care of physical properties personally connected with the deceased. It provides the widow and family an opportunity to relieve taut nerves a little with physical action. While functioning through such sad activity, those in grief gradually accept the actuality of the death.

I found this list on my sister's table when she was widowed last November. It will give you a partial idea of the diverse details, all of which mean decisions.

Things to do NOW:
1. Phone calls—his relatives—my relatives.
2. Decide time for funeral; discuss with funeral director.
3. Pick out casket.
4. Take clothes to funeral home. (Which suit?)
5. Ask funeral director if he puts notice in the paper or do I?
6. Get kids' clothes ready for funeral.
7. Flowers for funeral?
8. Call minister again. Songs? Scripture? Obituary?
9. Write into book names of people who brought food before I forget. Get dishes returned for today. Somebody help me!!
10. Take my dress to the cleaners.
11. Fix lesson plans at school for three days.

Things to do LATER:
1. Call lawyer.
2. Will?
3. Death certificate. Who needs them? How many?
4. Insurance?
5. Call Veteran's Administration.
7. What numbers do I take to Social Security office?
7. Find car title. Sticker runs out Monday.
8. Buy some thank-you notes (too high at funeral home).

It's healthy to begin to openly acknowledge death. Maybe we'll soon have common recognition of it. If we learn to share freely in a discussion of death, decisions can be made in advance, as a couple or as a family, and the widow won't have so many to make alone.

*"I can't go out to eat with you tonight. I
can't even eat!"*
—Comment made at a Solitaires meeting

What to Say and How to Help

The following pages seek to give guidance concerning unusual situations that may be encountered and to encourage more thoughtfulness in the choice and carrying out of commonly offered courtesies.

Unusual Situations

Widows whose husbands commit suicide have extra problems to contend with during their adjustment. It is hard for them to prevent strong feelings of guilt. Shame moves in to stay in many instances, and they decline to share their emotions at all.

We were sharing *how* our husbands died one evening. Widows need to tell it several times.

"My husband committed suicide," one widow said. She was new to the group.

"Have you had an extra burden of guilt?" I inquired.

"It's been so bad that this is the first time I've ever mentioned it to anyone. My husband died in another town. I told no one there and I've never mentioned it in the three years I've lived here. It's a sort of relief to have it out in the open."

This may be one of those areas where professional advice and counseling should be recommended.

"The bereaved should be encouraged to go for professional care any time they want to go," advises Dr. Mead. "It should be their own decision, but they should be encouraged or perhaps even coerced if the grief reaction seems inappropriate, particularly if it becomes unnaturally prolonged. Also, if the emotional reaction involves some really disturbed thinking, such as some delusional ideas, persistent confusion, or serious thoughts of suicide."

There are other unusual situations.

Sometimes our past is not as far behind us as we would like it to be. A woman who has been divorced for several years and is then notified of the death of her ex-husband still goes through the regular stages of grief, although time and distance may lessen the severity of her sadness.

More than emotions may be involved. One divorcée told us. "At my ex-husband's death I received a little money from an insurance policy. His second wife paid for some of the funeral expenses, but I was responsible for the burial." She was still held responsible even though it was ten years after the divorce.

"We hadn't seen him for years, but the children wanted to attend the funeral," another said. "I had to take them and it stirred up a lot of anger in me."

Another divorcée was in tears because she had just spent a week visiting with the man she had divorced many years ago. He was dying of emphysema. She still faces normal stages of grief.

Consider these unusual situations:

- What about those women who, if the truth were known, didn't even love their husbands and now have to fake sorrow? These widows probably feel guilty because of their true feelings.
- Think of the widow whose husband had a heart attack while involved in an affair. How will she handle that information, that anger, that guilt?
- Some widows may feel guilty about having been short on sexual participation with their husbands before death.
- What about the woman who initiates a divorce or leaves her husband, and then he dies before a final settlement or reconciliation is made? How will she handle the guilt?

Any widow carrying needless guilt should be advised to air her problem with a skilled listener or adviser. Such an adviser is usually not a friend or a family member. Professional counseling is not something to be avoided or put off until the widow is desperate. She needs to realize that her emotional and mental health are as important as her physical health.

79

Negative Comments

"Shape up. You probably would have had terrible problems with each other by the time the kids were teen-agers," one widow's cousin said.

"Most of us become widows at some time. You're just one sooner," Jeannine was told.

"That was supposed to comfort me?" she commented bitterly to us.

"Are you going to work right away?" Marge was asked by a girl friend the week of the funeral.

Marge commented, "I didn't have the slightest idea and wasn't ready to think about it. I wanted to be with my children—not working—besides, it was none of her business." Negative reactions were not normal for her. But right now she didn't *know* what she planned to do and was upset *because* she didn't know. Such questions, even if gentle and sincere, may fracture a fragile layer of resolve covering much doubt and indecision.

"One thing people said over and over which I could have done without was the statement, 'You must go on for the sake of your children.' As a mother I instinctively knew that. I didn't need constant reminders," Lisa said. She *was* a good mother and an efficient librarian. She knew what was right, but her nerves were strung tightly. It probably would have been better if her relatives and friends had just listened to her talk instead of giving advice.

In several cases widows were tempted to commit suicide but felt restrained because of responsibility for children. My own early teaching on morals, ethics, and religion probably prevented it for me, or maybe my love for my parents and my children helped keep me sane and sensible.

"You are young and pretty. You will get married again right away!" Eunice was told. (That's a little like saying to a child, "I'm sorry I ran over your dog. Let's go down to the pet store and buy another one.") The widow who was supposed to see some light in such a remark did, but it was the red light of anger. (She *has* married again, because she is a lovely, intelligent person and a fine mother—but the thought of remarriage was not acceptable to her on the day of the funeral nor anytime soon thereafter).

One widow's brother-in-law climbed into the car beside her for the ride back to town from the burial, took her left hand, tugged at her wedding band, and said: "You won't be needing those rings any more!"

Widows need gentle treatment and thoughtful care. Let's move on to think about proper ways of showing our concern.

Food

"Food is more than nourishment. Food means love and security to all of us and may have special symbolic value to different individuals. Certainly for the widow, food and appetite become very important in many little ways, particularly during the period of bereavement," Dr. Mead explained to me.

Members of our widow's discussion group agree that they appreciated food brought in by friends. We talked about our appetites, which disappeared with our husbands.

"I was pleased to find ice cream among the food supplied, for I didn't really care to eat and it slid down more easily than most foods when I was urged to try," Inez shared with us.

I had had not only Inez's problem but also an added psychological quirk of not being able to brush my teeth without vomiting my breakfast each morning.

"My mother has been here for a week now, busy all day and most of the evening running back and forth to the door, answering the telephone and keeping a record of flowers and food so I can send proper thanks later. Such a confused and complicated time!" Betty was busier than most widows, for she had more children.

Betty's comment describes conflicting emotions many new widows have when they become aware of the actions of friends trying to *help* them, and the reactions of loved ones who are trying to *protect* them from endless detail. Any new widow is obviously fatigued, although she may appear to function well. She is still in shock.

Widows appreciate people who take time to help them, but some ways are better than others. Maybe you'd like to consider the following ideas about furnishing food:

Label each bowl or pan. When several people are involved, decide in advance who will be designated to collect and take all the food in one trip to the home of the widow. Remember that it may be upsetting for a widow to have a stack of extra dishes around when everything in her life seems upside down anyway, regardless of her gratitude for the food. Returning bowls and pans when she has no energy is senseless, but she may feel obligated to add that chore to her lengthy list of details to handle.

You can help by stopping by to retrieve your own dishes, letting a designated person pick up all dishes in one or two visits, or by sending your food in a container marked disposable. If we prepare wisely, we can lessen the pressures on the widow.

Cards

A sympathy card is important as tangible evidence of love and concern. Usually they help. Once in a while they may hinder, despite the sender's best intentions.

I went to visit Sally. She shoved a batch of sympathy cards into my hands. I could tell by her slow movements and toneless speech that she was still in shock and had no idea what the cards said. Recalling my own experiences, I glanced through them.

"He is just away. . ." one said. Away implies return and even if Sally's heart didn't accept her husband's death completely yet, her mind was already beginning to know that it was final. Was the sender of that card fooling herself? She wasn't fooling Sally, or wouldn't very long.

What do sympathy cards really say? Well, to be honest, that *someone cares!* And that is important. But if you've lost someone dear recently, you probably look through the cards on the rack and read the verses more carefully than the average person.

Words that prove you care can be very simple!
"I'm thinking of you in this time of sorrow."
"I'm praying that God will comfort you."
"May God grant you peace."
Take time to recall the deceased and a pleasant time you shared. Think of a positive idea, attitude, or action of his that the widow and children would appreciate hearing about and sharing. Do you care enough to take the trouble to write it down for them? If so, add that note of cheer with the sympathy card. It will be reassuring for the family to reread later when the initial shock has passed.

A little sheet of notepaper with your honest feelings will be cherished after commercial printings are discarded and will probably be shared with growing children later. I still have such notes and letters even though it has been ten years since my husband died.

If you are a close friend and sincerely wish to be useful, write down an offer to help. Suggest your willingness to baby-sit, or to go out to eat with the widow, suggesting that she take advantage of the offer when she feels the need. Enclose it with your sympathy card or in a short encouraging note the next week, instead of telephoning to say, "What can I do to help?"

My mother died last summer. The card I appreciated most said:

> In the Loss of Your Loved One
> A chapter completed,
> A page turned,
> A life well-lived,
> A rest well-earned.

May you find peace in
the knowledge that your
loved one has completed but
one chapter in the Book of
Eternal Life.*

I noticed my eighty-year-plus father counted the cards that came each day as a detail to occupy his thoughts and time. He appreciated every card, but he laid aside a couple specifically regarding eternal life for me to see.

Transportation

We have seen that if the widow is older, with no children at home, or is new to the community, she may need your presence right away. She may also have a definite transportation problem and might welcome your offer to help her get out of the house, even for going to the grocery store.

One widow accepted a ride to a recent Solitaires meeting even though she had been blessed with a new car. "I'm uneasy because I haven't tried driving it yet, so I'm not adjusted to it," she said.

I know a wisp of a widow, past seventy years of age, who wears worn-out shoes because she wants a certain brand no longer made. She hasn't enough energy to ride a bus downtown or to shop at length, and she isn't willing to settle for less than the best. She won't even try the mail-order type anymore. Many widows like her need a patient chauffeur to help them run necessary errands.

---

*Quoted from a Hallmark card, Hallmark Cards, Kansas City, Mo. and used by permission.

The widow may have all she can manage being a mother, keeping up the home, chauffeuring children to music lessons, visiting the lawyer, and possibly seeing Social Security and Veteran's Administration officers.

Perhaps you can provide transportation for a child to Cub Scouts or Brownies for a month and help her save time and energy. She'll be able to cope better soon, and she will never forget your help.

People Can Help

Anyone who is willing to learn how to take the time to be supportive of a widow can help in innumerable ways. Little notes of encouragement from an acquaintance may be enough to cheer a widow through another day of adjustment.

Family members, if not too involved in personal grief stages, can be a special comfort to the widow who is trying to adjust.

Family Help

Grandparents, who have probably experienced the death of several loved ones, may be able to help more than anyone else at this time, especially if children are involved.

In our mobile society people often live across country from grandparents. Perhaps this is one reason why it is important to work toward extended families or adopted grandparents. This is a place for God's family to help the imcomplete human family.

It's sad that we have had to organize public social service groups to take over nearly every area in personal relationships and education that should be handled by family or church.

"What one thing has bothered you more than anything else about widowhood?" I asked a young widow who was left with two boys.

"I hope to be able to tell my brothers someday that they have disturbed me more than anything or anyone else. They will not get involved with my sons, not in any way. I need their help desperately. My sons need them even worse. A widower who has seven children of his own to care for has helped my older boy more than anyone else." I guess that widower's action would fall under the category of walking the second mile!

Widows and their children miss hearing a male voice and having male companionship. It would be wonderful if fatherless boys could have a man take them out for a ball game or to some sports event, especially during the first year. Organizations that help fill this need in our city are "Big Brothers" and "Big Sisters." They provide companionship for "one-parent" children.

A widow is misunderstood quite easily in our society if she seeks the help of anyone else's husband. Family members should understand this and offer their help whenever possible. The widow and her children will feel comfortable with brothers and brothers-in-law, if a good relationship exists. Although most widows can rear their children well, sons can sometimes present an added challenge. She would be greatly relieved to receive some help from an uncle or a grandfather. Friends who have sons near the same age as those of the widow would be invaluable if they would just take time to care.

Many married women, even relatives, worry needlessly that it isn't safe for a widow to be around their husband. Believe me, a widow isn't usually interested in anyone else's husband; she wants her own back. If couples befriend the widow together and they have a stable marriage, there won't be any problems. (Don't be surprised, however, if a widow becomes upset when a wife isn't appreciative of the man she has. Widows think it callous of a wife to mistreat what the widow believes to be a blessing.)

It would be naïve to assume that widows never become emotionally involved with men who try to help them. However, if laymen and male friends and relatives would reach out to the widow *together with their wives,* such problems could be avoided. Also, family members shouldn't rely on others to fulfill the obligations they should be handling. Such irresponsibility requires the widow to accept tempting help elsewhere. If a man who counsels a widow alone seems to fall in love with her, it was *not* a planned maneuver but rather something they both gradually allowed to happen because of their needs.

If we strive to love everyone with God's agape love, we will accept when we should and resist when we must. To me, that makes up the two parts of James 1:27: visiting the widow and keeping ourselves unspotted from the world.

Close Friends

Of all the things friends can do to help the widow, I'd like to emphasize the following, which is from a letter a pastor wrote to me:

We help our bereaved friends most when we help them deal with reality. Use the real words from the first day. Use the words 'dead' and 'died' instead of evasive phrases like 'passed away' and 'left.' Death is real. It really happened.

When you visit with the widow at death time or even months later in social situations, talk about her late husband. Use his name. It won't offend her. It honors him. She will enjoy having him recognized as a part of the group. She doesn't want him suddenly dismissed just because he is dead.

Perhaps a checklist here would be helpful in summarizing the ideas mentioned throughout this book:

- Write a note of cheer often. It can be as short as "I'm thinking of you and praying for your peace of mind."
- Buy her a copy of *Good Grief* and suggest that she read it.
- Help her plan something to look forward to.
- Have her and the children over for a meal.
- Be considerate in all your contacts; remember the normal stages of grief.
- Tell her to call anytime she is upset. (Nights are miserable.)

- Be a good listener.
- Offer to baby-sit if it seems advisable at all.
- Take the children out for entertainment.
- Take the whole family out for entertainment. (Children may be ready to go in advance of their mother.)
- Go visit after the first month if you live at a distance. (If she lost her husband in January, she will need your visit in June just as much as she did in January—probably more.)
- Don't be afraid to mention death and words that are related to it. (She isn't thinking of much else, anyway.)
- Don't assume that the widow wants your husband. (She wants her own back.)

The following poem expresses much of my feeling regarding friends of widows.

Why God Made Friends

God, in His wisdom, made a friend,
Someone on whom we can depend . . .
A loyal friend who'd understand
And always lend a helping hand.

He felt we'd need somebody who
Could comfort us when we feel blue . . .
Whose special warmth and happy smile
Would make us feel that life's worthwhile.

Someone with whom to take a walk,
To share a book or have a talk . . .
Who'd chat for hours on the phone
Or sense our need to be alone.

In short, God made a friend to be
Someone we're always glad to see.
There's little else that God can send
That means as much as one good friend.*

If the widow's children know you fairly well and
are old enough to understand, you might say to
them individually, in your own words:
"I am thinking about you as you adjust to a new
life without your father." Or, "I expect you have a
lot of questions you would like to ask somebody. I
have time and am willing to listen. Please feel free
to call me on the telephone or come over any time."
Listening is a good way for you to help the widow
or a young person. If the opportunity presents itself
in a natural way, you may want to suggest in your
own words that children:

- ask questions.
- talk to a teacher, counselor, minister, doctor, or
  almost anyone he or she would be comfortable
  with about feelings.
- try to abide by the rules of the house, even if
  Father isn't there to enforce them or Mother is
  too upset to notice.
- tell Mother "I love you."
- realize Mother's feelings will get better.
- realize that his or her own feelings will improve.

Maybe it will seem important to you to urge the
child not to:

---

*Greeting card verse published by permission of Paramount
Line, Inc., Pawtucket, Rhode Island.

- be afraid if Mother is ill. (Help the child realize that Mother won't die right away just because Father died.)
- feel ashamed about the loss of Father. (Let him or her know that you and others don't blame the child in any way. Perhaps you will want to actually verbalize the idea that it is not the child's fault.)
- feel guilty if he or she wished Father dead at some time. (Assure the child that Father didn't die because the child wished it—and the child is not to worry about it.)

Possibly you can let the child know that it is normal:

- to laugh.
- to cry.
- to hurt.
- to have nightmares.
- to question "why?"
- to wonder "why me?"
- to be temporarily mad at God.
- to be bitter.
- to hate someone connected with the death for awhile.
- to be upset with Father for leaving child and Mother.
- to be guilty about something said or done to a missing parent.

Let the child know that it is all right to have fun, to go on living, and to enjoy daily events when at all possible.

Facing the finality of a father's death takes time.

For a child gradually coming to believe that the death of a father is real, the larger unspoken psychological process of mourning would be something like this: "It's summer and Daddy is not here when I go swimming; it's fall and Daddy is not here when we eat Thanksgiving dinner; it's Christmas and Daddy is not here when we open the presents." Slowly a child accepts the repeated evidence of his senses and concludes to himself, "Daddy will not be here with me anymore." A similar process takes place for mourners of any age.[1]

Acquaintances

People who are not close friends can still provide necessary company and comfort for a widow when she is ready to reenter society.

"Call the widow on the telephone and ask when it would be convenient for you to come and visit. If she is reluctant, try again next week. Offer her some time out of the house for coffee and doughnuts or a Coke." Alice added her ideas to our widow's list of helpful things for friends to do. "When you are visiting, ask, 'May I do such and such to help you?' She is less likely then to avoid the offer, and you can tell by her expression if she really wished help but hasn't wanted to bother you."

"Yes, it's a blessing to have a friend offer to help do something specific and really mean it, instead of saying, 'Let me know if I can help you in any way.' I probably won't call the ones who put it that way," Zelma wearily related.

Let me explain what sometimes happens. When a

husband dies, friends and relatives rush to help the
widow. They are kind and generous with their
time. They share her grief, but the necessity of
providing for their own families calls them away.
She is left alone.

Then her shock melts away a small bit at a time
and painful awareness comes slowly. The loneliness becomes a heavy binding chain. A time comes
when undesired emotions surface, reactions grow
enormous, and she needs comforting friends. And
that is about the time some acquaintance says, "I
guess you have adjusted now!" (If you've experienced it you know more time is required to adjust
than people realize.)

"People can help by not being afraid of death, by
listening peacefully," Janice said at one of our
group meetings.

"To make widows and children feel more natural
and normal in society, continue having them in
your social groups," Brenda offered.

"If you think a widow needs help cleaning, offer
her your help or the name of a cleaning lady. It is
more important for me to spend time with my children than it is to sweep and dust." Sandra had five
children and her priority was proper, I believe.

Betty was newly widowed. Al refused to visit her
for three weeks although Betty's husband had been
his close business colleague. Why? Betty heard in-
directly later, "It upset Al too much just to think
about visiting you."

One of Jane's girl friends, whom she usually
shared an afternoon a week with, didn't show up for

a whole month after Jane was widowed. Jane found out later that her girl friend hadn't come or called because she didn't know what to say.

"Get your help from above instead of relying on your friends. I'd rather do it myself." This widow was resentful but she *would* manage.

"Although my husband's co-workers were very generous with gifts, cards, and offers of help, I didn't see any of them after the first week. This company had been a part of my life for twenty years, but this area of my life died with my husband. I'd like to have been included at least for a while," Rosella said.

Mary was offered companionship to help pass the hours, and she accepted and enjoyed her interests. She said, "The following summer I took up golf with my friend. This was great therapy."

"I was helped most by friends who had faith I could share," said Louise.

"Friends should absolutely stop asking the children what happened to their father and stop making pitying remarks to them," said Linda, trying to cope with widowhood and children.

I appreciated the friends who took me where I could hear good Bible teaching. Hearing God's promises made me feel I could manage to live again, rear my children, and do it all cheerfully, with His help.

Below are some Scripture verses widows have found helpful. The first two helped me most, initially.

The eternal God is thy refuge, and underneath are the everlasting arms (Deut. 33:27).

For the mountains shall depart, and the hills be removed; but my kindness shall not depart from thee, neither shall the covenant of my peace be removed, saith the Lord that hath mercy on thee (Isa. 54:10).

Trust in the Lord with all thine heart; and lean not unto thine own understanding. In all thy ways acknowledge him, and he shall direct thy paths (Prov. 3:5,6).

Be strong and of a good courage, fear not . . . for the Lord thy God, he it is that doth go with thee; he will not fail thee, nor forsake thee (Deut. 31:6).

Thou wilt keep him in perfect peace, whose mind is stayed on thee: because he trusteth in thee (Isa. 26:3).

I can do all things through Christ which strengtheneth me (Phil. 4:13).

With God all things are possible (Matt. 19:26b).

But my God shall supply all your need according to his riches in glory by Christ Jesus (Phil. 4:19).

---

[1]R.J. Lifton and E. Olson, *Living and Dying* (New York: Praeger, 1974), pp. 33–34.

"A child said, 'I'm afraid to be alone in the dark.' Mother said, 'You're not alone, you know. Jesus is with you.' The child answered, 'I know ... but I want someone with skin on.' "
—From *The Critical Moment* by Margaret Wold

9

Professionals Can Help

Physicians, ministers, and lawyers are usually the first professionally trained persons in contact with a widow after her husband dies. They are sometimes followed by counselors, psychotherapists, and psychiatrists.

Physicians come first because of the husband's death. The minister arrives next, to comfort. A lawyer deals with the legal affairs surrounding the death.

Physicians are dedicated to *saving* life, so death isn't easy for them to face either. Sometimes it's even threatening to them, a sign of failure.

Standing near a general physician and a psychiatrist, I overheard part of a question the physician asked: "Is it normal for a widow to ...." I realized that the subject of death is sadly neglected even in educated circles.

"Neither my physician nor my husband's physician notified me. It was someone else at the hospital who called." Arlene's voice hinted that she felt mistreated or cheated in some way.

Betty shared a positive experience with her physician. "I was glad he spoke honestly about what to expect regarding my husband's illness and the expected death."

"I needed to hear about the grief I could expect and the sexual desires I would feel later on," Sarah joined in. "My emotions were a surprise and I didn't understand them."

"All I needed was reassurance that I was normal," Sena said. "I could have handled the rest of it."

" 'I'm here when you or the children need me— just call,' was my doctor's only comment," Nancy told our group. "He squeezed my hand and shed tears. It was enough."

"My physician was inept, uninformed, and very self-conscious. He didn't spend enough time with me to be of any help," Beverly remembered.

"My physician told me a year after my husband's death —without even a checkup—that I was probably entering menopause. I was only thirty-seven. It was internal bleeding. We need to send more people to medical school if there aren't enough physicians to spend time with us. My time is as valuable as his—I resent those hours I have to wait." Ada was irate.

"Maybe if those who need psychologists would go to them, our physicians would have more time," Carol said.

"My physician discussed things openly and used medication wisely. I also saw a psychiatrist, who sent me to a counselor. Talking helped," Patricia said. Her open sharing about her psychiatrist helped others in the group accept the idea of obtaining professional, qualified assistance from a counselor with time to spend with them. (Much devastating advice is being given by non-Christian psychiatrists, psychologists, and counselors. We need Christian help. *Watch out*, dear reader!)

The physician or counselor dealing with a widow should probe sufficiently to unearth questions a widow naturally has but may be either reluctant to admit or unable to put into words.

He should be sure the widow understands the normal stages of grief. Does she know shock can easily upset her menstrual cycle for months? He should let her know the physical as well as the mental effects of shock, and he should warn the widow of the danger of mixing tranquilizers and alcohol.

A physician or counselor might suggest something pleasant for the widow to plan and look forward to during the months ahead. Is there a self-help therapy group in the area? She needs time to talk and assurance that her emotions are normal. Physicians or counselors could help get such a group organized; so could anyone else.

The function of the physician, lawyer, or minister should not end with the funeral. As time passes, these individuals can be instrumental in helping the widow develop new interests and activities. Also, they can caution her against things such as:

... get-rich schemes, the drink-a-lot club, the go-to-bed-a-lot club (for sex), and the rebound-marriage phenomena.

To be of real assistance to the widow, be kind, gentle, and caring. Imitate "Old Doc" from our nostalgic past. Everyone loved him. He didn't cure all of his patients, but he did care for a lot of folks. Cure when you can, but never stop caring for the patients. If you don't care, who will?[1]

Marian Champagne gave some good advice regarding physicians when she talked to widows about changes in the female body, depressions, and fears. "If you are going to one of those too-busy fellows or an old-timer who says, 'You just have to live through it,' get a new doctor and spare yourself and your children unnecessary suffering."[2]

Because of our technical legal system, the widow will need a lawyer's advice. Professional people don't usually criticize other professional people, especially within the same field. In fact, some professionals swear to an agreement that they will never verbally fault a co-worker. Widows are not bound by this code.

Our group agreed that lawyers should not be expected to be genuinely concerned for one's welfare, nor to offer advice outside their field. My lawyer gave me some good advice, but I wouldn't listen. I wish I had bought land as he had suggested, instead of so many mutual funds in the stock market. My best profit came on a city lot.

Other widows share their experiences:

"The trust department at the bank, who were executors as set up by my husband and the lawyer, advised me to invest. I did it my way, and now I think maybe the money was too easy to get to; but all in all, I feel I did the very best I could with what strength I had. I was encouraged to go back to my job, but I wasn't able physically. I can see my mistakes now, but looking back I know I did the best I could then."

"Things are going to go wrong around the house. Expect it. Try not to fall apart when it happens. The stool will need to be unplugged. The motor will go out on the humidifier. The garage door opener won't work—and they don't even carry the part anymore. These are not earthshaking things, but they are upsetting when you don't have a man around to take care of them for you. The lawyer won't help on these things. You'll think everyone is trying to take advantage of you. They may be—but probably it is just that you are alone and your nerves are ragged. It's really irritating when people aren't doing their jobs well and even the bank has your account number mixed up with an old outdated one you had years ago. Expect things like that."

"If someone approaches you about a way to invest your money, say, 'That's a great idea. Talk to my lawyer (or trust officer) about it!' "

"My lawyer told me how to invest my insurance proceeds and I appreciated it," Ellie told us.

"My lawyer drew up a will for me here at home. I didn't like the last page where it said I must come to him with the estate. So I tore up the will and got a second lawyer. He drew up a will I liked, but he saw me coming and charged me $250. Watch out for lawyers," Velma, a middle-aged widow, warned.

My sister's husband said he had been to see the lawyer and had made a will. He hadn't. He said he had sent in the income-tax forms, forging her name. He hadn't. He said they had important papers in the safety deposit box. It didn't even contain a paper clip or a rubber band. He said some money he had borrowed from their son was in a special savings account in a nearby town. He had withdrawn the money. *Her* car was in *his* name. There was *NO* life insurance. She could have bought that for her husband. Women who want to avoid trouble will check on these things.

"There should be a way to have some bonds in your own name that the lawyer wouldn't get a percentage of—maybe in a special box somewhere," Faye said.

"It's no blessing that a lawyer's motivation is mercenary rather than merciful," an older widow said.

"Some lawyers can be helpful. They are not in business to relieve grief, and widows should be the first to realize that. I just happened to find someone who compatibly handled my business," one of the younger widows said. She was from a small town, which may have been an advantage.

"Our company lawyers helped us handle all the paperwork and it has really been great," agreed two widows whose husbands were both killed at the same time in a plane crash.

Sandra and her physician husband were able to plan details about his death after accepting his terminal illness. Sandra and Henry visited their lawyer three months prior to Henry's death so that they would both know how money matters should be settled.

Sandra called her lawyer three days after the funeral. He was in town but not at the office, and he didn't return her call. Finally a week later, feeling guilty but frustrated, she called his home and talked to his wife. Sandra learned that others were also upset because he hadn't answered their telephone calls.

He has a right to a vacation, but it was irritating to Sandra to learn that he runs horses in the races, which last most of May, June, and July. She told us, "I sent husband Henry an air-mail letter by way of heaven today. I put thirty cents on it. I said to him, 'I told you in advance this lawyer was too slow!' "

Sandra's sense of humor and her verbalization released tension. Still, her lawyer's behavior was unacceptable.

"It isn't fair for lawyers to take advantage of widows," Sally burst out. "Many do since they know the widow doesn't have enough energy to begin again with another lawyer. Who wants to explain all those details again when she is having trouble talking about her husband's death at all? Lawyers may be busy, but so is the widow. She is also worn out and wondering about income for living. Some lawyers wonder why people feel a negative attitude toward them. No one else in the world gets away with this type of behavior; why should the lawyer?"

A friend of mine worded it more carefully: "I

have become convinced that lawyers, of all professional people, have the least amount of personal concern and sensitivity! It must be one of the areas of training that seems unnecessary to law school curriculum."

I'd like to suggest reading the book *"What Every Woman Doesn't Know"*[3] to learn about wills, estates, the I.R.S., inheritance taxes, and more. It is particularly helpful for the problems of women whose husbands were not wealthy.

Obviously, because of bad experiences with lawyers, many widows believe *all* lawyers are cold and insensitive. This, of course, is not true. However, the widow should, if possible, meet with her lawyer together with a knowledgeable and trusted friend. She should also remember that the lawyer is a legal advisor—nothing more. For emotional and spiritual help the widow needs to go elsewhere.

In my experience, the pastor and his wife are the most willing couple available for help. They are also the most overworked, underpaid, and least appreciated. (It's not fair to expect them to wait for a proper reward in heaven!)

"My preacher came and cried with me many times," was one widow's way of expressing her gratitude.

Another widow said, "I need to work at something. But my faith is too personal a thing to talk about." Bless her heart, if it isn't personal it's not worth much. Mine is personal, too, but it's definitely worth sharing with others.

"Christ is the answer. I needed Him but I just didn't know it," Grace said after she learned to rely on Him.

"My priest came a lot at first, but he was afraid we would learn to depend on him, so he quit coming," Reba said. She *needed* someone to visit with, and none of her friends seemed to know how to help. She said she didn't try to help herself adjust for more than four years.

"I think maybe women should be helped before they are widows. Perhaps a sermon now and then on preparing for such a shock would be good," one widow suggested.

"My minister treated our situation realistically," reflected Helen. She didn't run from her problems, and she appreciated the help she received.

"A pastor should admit the widow's loss for what it is and not try to justify it. 'It is God's will' is not a sufficient statement for a woman in grief," Betty said with bitterness.

"He should not push and pry," said Josephine. I don't know what happened between Josephine and her spiritual guide, but this statement points up how sensitive a widow is when her whole world seems upset.

Sometimes a widow turns around words intended for comfort in a way no one could anticipate. "If everyone is going to love everyone else in heaven, then I don't want to go. I don't want other women loving my husband. He is mine," Jan said. Of all the people I have met who have read Catherine Marshall's *To Live Again*, Jan is one of the few who did not like it.

"The thing my rabbi said that was most helpful was, 'Live one day at a time.' I found out you can do that!" Several widows nodded in agreement with Shirley's encouraging words.

"Our preacher said, 'You are adequate and can rear your family!' I appreciated that reassurance," Wanda spoke quietly. She always listened but didn't talk much in our group.

"I wouldn't have taken kindly to a rhetorical recital of God's goodness at that time." The speaker was a very mature person with much faith.

Janice absorbed much comfort from her pastor. "He came immediately when I called and came back later in the evening when the undertaker was here for preliminary planning. He called several times prior to the funeral. That helped me."

"Something helpful he *could* do would be to call back later after my immediate grief to discuss the whys, eternal life, and my confusion of thoughts," Kelli pointed out. She had been doing something common to most widows: asking questions concerning life after death.

Many people have negative feelings about the church. But when a death occurs almost every person is willing to recognize the pastor as the proper one to handle the situation.

"Impress on priests that Christian faith will help more than anything," one widow wrote on a questionnaire regarding advice she would like to give to spiritual leaders.

If pastors aren't new in their profession, they have already set up patterns for helping people through the maze of emotions that follow the death of someone they love. Concerned lay people can do almost anything the pastor can and may have more time to do it.

Remember that the widow seeks comfort and reassurance. She usually receives encouragement first from the pastor. However, Christian pastors, counselors, and laymen have incomplete training unless they have a thorough knowledge of the Scriptures regarding death, resurrection, heaven, and so on. Most of us who are widows know from helping others or from our own experience that ministers who really have a thorough knowledge of the mysteries of death and the hereafter are rare.

I was one of the widows who could totally accept myself as soon as I realized God loved me just as I was. The assurance of His love gave me energy to begin to improve the areas I felt were lacking.

Here are some of the questions widows ask and their scriptural answers:[4]

1. *What is man?*
The Word says man is made up of three parts. God "formed man of the dust of the ground" (body), "breathed into his nostrils the breath of life" (spirit), and "man became a living soul" (soul). (See Genesis 2:7, 1 Thess. 5:23, and Heb. 4:12.)

It helps so much to know that our body is not really "us." Our body is only our house, or temporary dwelling place, while we are here on earth.

We live in a body, we are a soul, and we have a spirit. The soul is the personality. It is the part of us that contains our mind or intellect, the part of us that can reason and remember. It includes our emotions or feelings and also our ability to choose or make decisions. It is this part of us that decides whether or not to do right or to go our own selfish way. (See 2 Cor. 5:1-10.) The dictionary helps explain the word "soul."

For the Christian, spirit is the part of us which

Scripture calls "the dwelling place of God's Spirit" (1 Cor. 3:16). This is the part of us through which God communicates with us (Rom. 8:16).

2. *What is death?*

When a person dies, only the body dies. As Christians, our spirits and souls will live forever with God. In Exodus 3:6 God spoke to Moses, saying, "I am the God of thy father, the God of Abraham, the God of Isaac, and the God of Jacob." God listed men who were dead in body, but indicated they were as alive as Moses. He is a living God and a God of living men.

At death then, the body dies and the spirit and soul depart from it. I like 2 Corinthians 5:8 because it tells me that as soon as I am absent from this body I am present with my Lord! Hallelujah!

3. *What happened to my husband? Where did he go?*

"And Jesus said unto him, Verily I say unto thee, today shalt thou be with me in paradise" (Luke 23:43).

You may also check out Matthew 8:11, 25:34; John 12:26, 14:2,3; Hebrews 11:6,10,16, 13:14; and 1 Peter 1:4.

4. *I know my husband was a Christian, and so he went to heaven; but what is it like there?*

"And the building of the wall of it was of jasper: and the city was pure gold, like unto clear glass" (Rev. 21:18).

See also Hebrews 11:10, 13:14; 1 Corinthians 2:9; and Acts 7:55,56.

5. *Is he conscious or asleep?*
"Whosoever liveth and believeth in me shall
never die" (John 11:26). See also Matthew 19:29,
22:32, 17:1-3, and John 5:24, 11:25,26.

6. *Does he have a body?*
". . . Reach hither thy finger, and behold my
hands; and reach hither thy hand, and thrust it into
my side: and be not faithless, but believing" (John
20:27-28). So Jesus has a body.
See also 1 Corinthians 15:40-44, Luke 24:33-43,
John 20:11-16, and Acts 10:40-41.

7. *What about the resurrection?*
"And this is the will of him that sent me, that
every one which seeth the Son, and believeth on
him, may have everlasting life: and I will raise him
up at the last day" (John 6:40).
There is no such thing as a "spiritual resurrection." The spirit does not die. See also Colossians
3:4, 1 John 3:2, John 6:44, John 5:25-29, and 1 Corinthians 15:20-22.

8. *Will we know each other in heaven?*
"And I say unto you, that many shall come from
the east and the west, and shall sit down with Abraham, and Isaac, and Jacob, in the kingdom of
heaven" (Matt. 8:11).
See also Matthew 17:1-3 and Luke 16:19-31.

9. *What will we do in heaven?*

"He that overcometh shall inherit all things; and I will be his God, and he shall be my son" (Rev. 21:7).

See also Revelation 3:21, Luke 12:32, 1 Peter 1:4, and Revelation 19:1.

To answer some of those questions (at least as much as we can know from Scripture) brings immeasurable comfort to a grief-stricken widow.

A pastor should pray with her and try to call weekly the first month, on the telephone if not in person. Spend at least two hours with her *and her family* to answer questions right away, and then schedule a time later when the shock has lessened and more questions plague her and her children.

To anyone giving spiritual guidance: Don't be afraid of tears or assume she'll crack up if you are sympathetic. She may need to cry. A widow remembers who helps her most at this critical time in her life.

If you are helping a widow and she says, "I don't like God today," don't say, "Oh, come on now. You *can't* feel that way." She can and she does! Accept it and remember it is transitory. God understands. He can take it!

Remember that thoughts of eternity are of great importance to her right now. (Consider the plight of those who have no hope!)

Ask the widow what would comfort her. She has expectations. You can't know her background entirely. I *wanted* to hear comforting Scripture and have a prayer.

It's normal to feel unqualified to deal with death

when you haven't experienced the loss of a close loved one. But pray before you go. Let the Holy Spirit guide you as to what to say.

My college minister, G. L. Messenger, and I were conversing years later about people not knowing what to say to the bereaved. He shared this story with me concerning himself.

"We had just moved into a new city when a son of a couple on our block was killed. Although they didn't belong to our church, I visited them several times to comfort them. But I never knew what to say.

"Each time I left their home and walked down their front walk, I mentally kicked myself for not having said more.

"I kept returning, thinking each time that I would improve and be able to say something comforting.

"Months later a mutual friend shared a comment from the couple with my wife. 'We felt his love and concern just by his presence and we appreciated his visits more than anything anyone tried to do for us.' "

Ministers should encourage the congregation to help widows, especially during the lonely holiday seasons. Weekends, anniversaries, and birthdays are hard for a widow, as is watching a child graduate from high school, even years later, without her husband's presence.

Don't assume with everyone else that the widow is well adjusted in five months just because she seems calm and manages to smile. Her worst possible moments may be yet to come. The whole first year is traumatic.

"Your family is all around you and I know you're feeling fine," was a comment heard by a new widow a month after her husband died. (This kind of comment accentuates the hurt and loneliness, and underlines the widow's feeling that no one understands.)

"Not true," the widow shared with us, "because I wasn't."

One word of caution: What she tells you is confidential, especially in small towns.

Personally, I believe it would be good for pastors to find time to get acquainted with every member of their congregations so they can be of comfort when a problem arises. It isn't normal for anyone to put a lot of trust in a near stranger or to go to them with personal problems.

Rev. J. Keith Cook has spent many hours helping our widow's self-help therapy group organize and function.

Another pastor put the following notice in the Sunday bulletin and made those who responded aware of opportunities:

HANDY MAN

The Community Action Committee is looking for a few good men who are handy at fixing things around the house. Any type of skill is acceptable. We have widows and others who need help in this way and are not able to do it themselves. BE A GOOD GUY AND HELP!

Clergymen and their congregations can offer invaluable help to widows and their families, but it takes an investment of one's time and energy.

[1]David W. Bean, M.D., "On Helping Widows" (a paper given to general practitioners, Creighton University, Omaha, Nebraska, 1975).

[2]Marian Champagne, *Facing Life Alone: A Legal Guide for Widows and Divorcées* (Indianapolis: Bobbs-Merrill, 1974), p. 201.

[3]Gustave Simons, *What Every Woman Doesn't Know* (New York: Macmillan, 1964).

[4]Adapted from an unpublished study on widowhood by Jeanette Collins, Bible teacher and Christian counselor. Used with permission.

"The first year is the hardest."
—Comment made at a Solitaires meeting

10
As Months Pass

The best description of widowhood I have heard
came from Rev. Keith Cook. "If you take a sharp
object and slice a married woman in two, toss one
half away and say to the remaining part 'HEAL—
AND FUNCTION,' you have an adequate description of how the widow feels and an idea of the
length of time it will take to heal." You can surmise
from his example that there will be scars forever,
the need for tenderness a long time, and a lengthy
period of adjustment.

I didn't really cry for five months, and wasn't
over the trauma in six. Then, too, there were some
things I began to miss besides my husband.

When I was widowed, I appreciated hearing
business-oriented dialogue from my husband's
dental friends and classmates. It was our main interest for so many years that I began to yearn for it

after I quit attending dental-related functions. My friends there still welcomed me, but I began to feel out of place.

One lawyer's wife shared with our widow's group: "My husband was in a large corporation. After his death it was hard to hear any conversation comparable to what I was used to and I felt totally ignored."

"There was no way I could actually hear rail-road-connected discourse anymore, and that was like cutting off my right arm," another woman said.

Most of the hallucinations (perceptions or impressions not founded in reality) are over by the end of six months. But strange things happen at first.

"I knew he was lying right beside me on the bed."

"I felt my husband put his hand on my shoulder when I was sitting in my rocking chair. I know in my mind that he said, 'I'm all right!' "

"He made love to me in my dream, and it was very satisfying."

We have talked with widows concerning what helped most in overall adjustment:

"My mood lifted most when people told me about something good my husband had done for them."

"I liked most having friends listen without condoning or condemning."

"Telephone calls from out-of-town friends, special invitations from friends, or just forcing myself to get out of the house to visit a close friend or shut-in lifted my mood the most."

"Finding something I enjoyed doing and keeping busy helped me."

"Keeping in touch with considerate friends and relatives. (But my telephone bill really went up.)"

Two negative comments were repeated frequently: "Let's face it: We live in a couple-oriented society and without a husband and his position, you're usually dropped."

"The thing that depressed me most was going places I had been with him, especially where we had first dated or had had a particularly good time."

Very few widows are able to say they have kept their own original circle of couples friends—especially by the end of the first year. Some will naturally seek out other widows to share experiences with, but much of the change in the friendship circle will not be something the widow wished to have happen. They are usually just uncomfortable with couples.

Moods change. Don't be surprised if a widow promises to come for dinner and then calls during the day or even at the last minute to say she can't come after all. Feelings fluctuate up and down like a car on a steep roller-coaster. The fear she feels at the thought of being with you, combined with her own emotions—for a whole evening—may seem too much for her.

If you have proven your ability to face your own emotions, can talk to her about death, and aren't afraid of and won't be distressed at seeing or sharing her tears, she will be more comfortable with you than with anyone else in the world.

One of the nicest things you can do for her is to

give her something to look forward to. If she can't manage something on the day she agreed to, set a new date while she is apologizing and let her plan on it. She may put you off several times. Do call again and don't be offended.

"I thought it was easier for older women to learn to live alone," a widowed student nurse informed us during a Solitaires meeting. "I learned I was wrong about that."

Actually, older women may be more lonely than younger ones. Many of them have no family nearby, are unable to drive, hate to ask for help, fear getting out at night, are not free to spend money for lunch with friends, are afraid to venture out on ice and snow, have never learned to travel by air, dislike driving in traffic, don't know the way to the airport, haven't heard of guaranteed reservations, have never rented a car in a strange city, and have never taken the leadership role in any area outside the home.

"I was glad a widow told me not to make hasty decisions and not to openly discuss the amount of insurance money I received. I would have made some regrettable errors," Jennifer said.

Kathy wrote on her questionnaire regarding medicinal help. "Maybe a few sleeping pills will help to get the rest necessary to see one through the immediate ordeals. After that, willpower must take over if one is to make a normal recovery. Work until the body is physically tired. That's the best remedy. Do for others and forget oneself. Pills are crutches which should not be used. We might as well take all the hurt full blast. The shock wears off slowly anyway. When one hurts enough and long enough, the body just naturally gets tired and rest comes. After rest, the hurt begins again, but in time it eases little by little. Maybe a numbness takes the place of the ache and hurt, but that eventually goes too. Pills and alcohol only retard nature's healing process."

We don't all agree on what is best, but I believe being calm and able to sleep are vital to well-being. I see nothing wrong with tranquilizers and sleeping for a very short time. God made physicians and medicine, too. But let me warn you to use caution, for there is real danger here. Too many of us think of addiction in the same terms we think of death or widowhood: It can't happen to me.

Some widows seem unable to release their husbands and therefore cling to physical things that are connected to him some way in their minds and memories. Two middle-aged widows experienced the death of an older family pet in the past year, and it became rather traumatic because each had shared enjoyment of their dogs with their deceased mates. It was as if a final string were cut.

Linda shared a couple of ideas on her questionnaire: "I saw two widows in particular who left an impression on me. One grieved at the grave until it was almost disgusting. Another was under such heavy sedation that she didn't realize what was taking place or who was at the funeral. I had vowed then that I would never be that way."

I, too, had watched a cousin grieve by visiting her husband's grave every day for months.

"I feel that with the help of God and friends around, one can manage not to mourn on and on for sympathy. Early days were the easiest for me. It was the days and weeks of loneliness later and coming home to an empty house that made it difficult for me. I'd heard about the loneliness, but I didn't believe it or really feel it until it happened to me," Betty said. Nearly all widows agree about loneliness *months* after the funeral.

"I lacked interest and desire to live for some time," is probably the least expressed but most dominant feeling among widows. A woman who is very mature, was widowed twice, and married a third time wished to tell church members this: "Just don't forget the widow and children for the first year. Include them in gatherings when at all possible. Keep them busy and get them out and around. Children adjust faster than widows because they are more active and out with friends more."

One gallant lady said, "It was easier the second time I was widowed as I had a child to care for then."

Knowing the widow who said the following almost makes me believe she remembers it the way it really was—but not quite. "I've always kept busy and *never* allowed depressions to take root."

A younger widow shared: "It's as if someone lifted up the edge of a rug, swept my husband underneath, then put it back down, hiding him completely. Friends don't want to talk about him. It's as if he never existed. I feel as if I'm losing my mind, but I know he lived, for I have one of his children here beside me and another due soon. I was pregnant when he died."

"Holidays are the worst," Betty confided. "We had good times as a family. It was tough to live through our wedding anniversary. I had a hang-up about our wedding vows being severed."

I cried on Mother's Day, although it was the father of the family we had lost. It seemed humorous, but I wasn't laughing.

"The way I've changed most is by becoming more independent. I am probably less trusting of businessmen, such as lawyers and mechanics, now. I keep trying to convince myself that I can handle my new life."

"Now that I have passed the first anniversary of his death, I think it is going to be easier to stop reliving every little event or experience we ever shared." Somehow it does work this way.

Widows have also shared experiences regarding sex, dreams, and nightmares. Several have received release from sexual frustrations by a vivid dream that seemed to include orgasm.

Dreams and nightmares may occur for years and may comfort or upset. Whichever feeling follows will probably last longer than usual.

My own early dreams included finding my husband alive but unable to talk. Even after I remarried three years later, he would reappear in my dreams, laughing and loving me. The most recent dream was just this year, ten years after I was widowed. I saw him with the Lord Jesus, and they were both laughing.

Another widow shared the following experience: "My husband was in an accident, was unconscious two weeks, and then died. My nightmares about him and the hospital were so real that I was in tears and nearly paralyzed for several days. Finally a Christian friend said, 'Have you asked the Lord to protect your unconscious mind from the terrible nightmares you are having?' I prayed about it and from that day on, I never had another one."

Another widow tells the most important thing she has learned by being widowed. "I've learned that material things mean nothing. I would give everything I have to get him back, but that is impossible. I now believe in living each day to the fullest and telling tomorrow to take care of itself."

"We attempt to conceal what we can neither face nor escape."
—R.J. Lifton and E. Olson in *Living and Dying*

11

Society, Customs, and Preparation

We could all adjust more easily to death if our parents had discussed death with us before we reached adulthood. Have you talked to your children?

Girls and boys who have heard their parents talk about funerals, adjusting to new situations, and working through the normal stages of grief will find it more natural to admit there is such a thing, think about it, and accept it when it comes.

Fathers and mothers who can talk about death with calmness and confidence will not have to be in a quandary regarding questions about death and eternity when they are drowning in a sea of sorrow.

The subject of death can be taught to children as soon as they begin to ask questions. At least by seven years of age they are old enough to understand. (In Chapter 9 you will find a list of scriptural references regarding death.) Here are a few things you can share with them.

1. *Man* is made up of three parts—spirit, soul, and body. We are a soul, we live in a body, and we have a spirit. We are told in Scripture that our body is merely the house we live in while on earth. When we die (if we are a Christian) we receive a new body like Jesus received after His resurrection.

We may tell them the soul is the personality, the thing that makes us individually different from anyone else. It is our mind, our memory, our feelings, and the ability to choose and make decisions. The Spirit is the part of us where Jesus lives when we receive Him into our life. This is one way we hear His voice and know that He loves us.

2. *Death* is merely passing from our earthly body into our heavenly body. We will be just as much alive then as we are now, only perfect and beautiful. We might compare it to the caterpillar and the butterfly. The lowly little worm can only crawl at first and is quite ugly in comparison to the brilliantly colored butterfly that emerges, goes soaring freely into the air, and leaves the old body behind.

3. *Heaven* is where Christians go after they die. What is it like there? Jesus said, "In my Father's house are many mansions: if it were not so, I would have told you. I go to prepare a place for you. . . . I will come again, and receive you unto myself; that where I am, there ye may be also (John 14:2,3).

If we can love and have faith in Jesus to save us, surely we can trust Him to prepare a delightful place for us.

I believe that every child should be taken to a funeral early in life, preferably that of a not-so-familiar friend or relative, so that the experience won't turn out to be a first-timer when his father dies, as happened with my boys. Our second family funeral was, for my four children, that of a fun-loving grandfather and my two boys were asked to be pallbearers. Was it surprising that one vomited during the eight-hour ride home? Not at all.

You are protecting them, you say? Death can be very upsetting if you have never personally come in contact with it in your entire life. (Losing a pet during your childhood is not really a similar experience, in my opinion.)

Another opportunity for sharing death-connected conversation could be when a child returns to school after attending the funeral of a parent. However, many teachers don't know how to communicate with children who have lost a parent. Where in our death-ignoring nation could teachers learn how to make it a learning situation in the classroom? (Yes, we watch it constantly on TV, but that's not the same as having it happen to us.)

I was blessed because my youngest son had an understanding widow for a teacher when his daddy died.

I taught school for more than a dozen years, and I never talked, or was encouraged to talk, about how to deal with death.

The tribulation of those adjusting to the death of a loved one could easily be discussed during high school, sociology, psychology, or family life courses. We have several concerned home economics teachers in Nebraska who have invited widows to share their experiences with young people in family life classes. Many of our doctors, lawyers, and ministers admit they didn't receive the training they need in this area. I wish I could have had the opportunity of hearing from firsthand experience earlier in my life.

Young people are interested in learning about death. They have thoughtful questions and are not afraid to ask them. Do you recall feeling that death was a long way off when you were a teen-ager? In my mind it was *just as distant* at age thirty-six, but in reality it was very close for my husband of forty.

The youngest widow who has come to our self-help group was widowed at age twenty-one. She had been married only six months, which reinforces the idea that no time is too soon to discuss dying and the dynamics of doing what we can to ease the emotions of those who are left.

"It's appropriate to be inadequate" is a beautiful statement. It may be applicable in comforting a widow who has not learned how to function after her loss. But we don't *have* to be deficient in dealing with the circumstances surrounding death. I believe the modern woman is interested in being *very* adequate.

Laura was a radiant bride when she recently married Dan under the redwood trees in her parents' lovely yard. Families and friends watched as they looked into each others' eyes and recited original vows.

If we visit with Laura in ten years, will she be

wiser than most of us were about facing death?
Let's hope so! Perhaps she will never have to share,
as some widowed women have, the following experience:

"I cheerfully greeted my husband at the end of a
busy day, intending to discuss with him what I
should do if he were to die. But I changed my mind.
I said to myself, 'I won't upset him with such a
morbid topic.' I wish I had."

Will Laura discuss death with Dan? Or will she,
because of a lack of confidence in discussing this
area of life, be as unprepared to deal with her husband's death ten years from now as she was when
she was a bride?

Will Dan be receptive if Laura mentions death?
Many wives get a negative response when they try
to talk about wills or widowhood. A wise couple
will agree on details regarding burial location and
arrangements, even if the uncomfortable conversation is brought about by having attended a crema-
tion or a burial. Since we aren't comfortable with
the subject, we usually put it aside at the smallest
interruption with a sigh of "glad-that's-over" relief.
Our way of erasing things from our minds is amaz-
ing.

Imagine yourself in the midst of tremendous confusion, in shock, unable to think clearly regarding
your future and your finances—and having to decide what amount to pay for a casket and where to
pick a burial plot. Should you sell your home and
move to something smaller, perhaps an apartment
more easily cared for by one person?

Having had little or no conversation with your

partner regarding these things to draw upon as a reference point makes your situation worse. Widowhood isn't a pleasant song to sing. But its plaintive tune is unexpectedly repeated like a ruined record—over and over and over throughout our nation.

Wouldn't it be better to discuss expensive decisions with your partner, even though it gives you an uneasy feeling, while loving arms are still here to hold you warmly and securely? Any widow can tell you the answer to that question.

We have been so busy making progress that we have rushed past some older, wiser habits that were very good. We have not only departed from them but discarded them entirely.

"People rarely mourn for a year any more, but there was considerable psychological wisdom in the tradition prescribing that length of time, say the authors of *Living and Dying*.[1]

In our part of the world, we have resisted the custom of wearing black clothing, and we have thrown away the black armband, too. Both were sensible outward signs of inner grief, helping others to identify with us.

We have even rushed one step further—into the make-believe world of the ostrich. We have firmly buried our heads in the sand. We have sand in our ears and won't hear about death; sand in our eyes and can't see it. We have breathed in sand, so that our lungs and brains refuse to function efficiently in this area.

Even literature about death is abrasive to our

minds, like sandpaper, so we throw it in the trash. "Take it away so we can forget," we say.

I tried ignoring death for thirty-seven years, but there came a day when I couldn't!

To paraphrase, "I have seen the enemy and she (or he) is me!" We hinder ourselves.

Joseph Newman expressed it well in his book for men: ". . . the subject matter is bound to be disturbing to her. (Before you grow impatient or upset yourself, do not overlook your own delay in approaching the topic because you did not want to face it straight on!)"[2]

If you are a married man, allow yourself to picture your own wife as a widow. You will probably have to force yourself to do it. What can you do now to help her adjust her daily thinking and what discussion or action that includes her now would make things easier for her in the days of widowhood if you were to die next month?

The following is a partial list of what I *wish* my husband had done before he died. Maybe my hindsight can be your foresight!

I wish my husband had

. . . made a will. Joseph Newman has a well-organized checklist on family affairs in the back of the book he compiled. I suggest you study it.

. . . discussed funeral services, cost, and necessities with me. I would have been visibly upset at the time, but I can see now that it would have eased the pressure I felt while making decisions when I was in shock after his airplane crashed.

. . . bought two plots at the cemetery. We were settled and had no plans to move in the near future because of our own private business, so it would have been a sensible purchase. Our shared choice then would have been wiser than mine over the telephone from out-of-state later.

. . . filed loan and mortgage papers, Social Security and Veteran's Administration information, our marriage certificate, birth certificates for the whole family, and all of our car papers with the life insurance policies he had, so I would have been saved a search. I couldn't find all of the dates and numbers I needed for the Veteran's Administration and the Social Security officers immediately. That was an unnecessary headache. It was upsetting enough to have to repeat the birth dates for four children plus Charlie's over and over.

I've been told by one military widow that the personnel department sends a yearly notice to each serviceman ordering him to update his folder, put things in order, and indicate by a signature that he has completed a will.

Frequently, women have refused not only to discuss death with their husbands but also to read a pamphlet or scan an article of any kind on the subject. This turning away from truth only makes shock more severe when we are faced with a mountain of demanding details as a new widow.

Maybe a good way to prepare is to ask yourself for one whole day, "What will I do about *each* detail regarding *everything* my husband usually does—if he isn't here and won't be ever again?" Then try thinking those thoughts for a week. (It will help your marriage; you'll begin to appreciate him anew!)

Ask yourself such things as:

- Could I write the checks and balance the checkbook?
- Do I know where to take the car for repair?
- Who could I call to help a child in trouble with the law?
- What company could I count on to unplug the plumbing in the middle of the night?
- How will I spend my evenings for a whole month if I have no partner?
- What interests do I have that don't depend on the fact that I am married?
- How long will my money last?

Don't hide from it—think about it!

Women who adjust best to widowhood are those who learned or could have learned to act independently in advance. You can think and plan without ruining your role as a wife or his role as leader. There's even a chance that you won't be widowed so soon if you relieve some of his pressures by taking care of more details now.

Lily Pincus expressed it well when she wrote, "The women who come to my notice because they need help to cope with the adjustment to widowhood are likely to be those who were never sure of their true selves, whose identities always depended on others. The crisis of bereavement highlights their inner situation."[3]

I asked some Omaha widows what advice they have for wives who still have husbands. Here are some of their comments:

"I feel that if women realized how suddenly everything could be over, no time would be lost in anger or jealousy."

"I think a wife should tell herself, 'This could happen to me.' Although it would be impossible to thoroughly imagine herself in such a situation, she could probably prepare herself some. Also, it might help her in understanding a friend's needs."

"Treat each day as it comes. Be honest with yourself. Appreciate your man—he may be gone tomorrow."

"I can't stand women who gripe about their husbands when I don't even have one anymore. They should appreciate what they have at the moment."

"Everyone always has advice to give. Do what you feel is right for yourself, even if your friends shake their heads in wonder."

"Learn about business details that affect you so you won't be at a complete loss."

"I'd outline all plans to use in case of his death."

"Remember, time does help to ease the pain of heartbreak."

"If you become widowed, stay home and become well-adjusted yourself. It will help lessen the problems your children will have."

"Some women adjust more easily with a paid job or some volunteer work to pass the time."

You are doing yourself no favor by living as if death will never affect you, and you will be of little help to a widow who has had to stop pretending.

[1]R. J. Lifton and E. Olson, *Living and Dying* (New York: Praeger, 1974), p. 33.

[2]Joseph Newman, ed., *Teach Your Wife How to Be a Widow* (Washington, D.C.: U.S. News and World Report, 1973), p. 25.

[3]Lily Pincus, *Death and the Family: The Importance of Mourning* (New York: Pantheon, 1975), p. 203.

*"It's the total loneliness that becomes
nearly unbearable."*
—Author

12

A Split in the Union

We are created with a capacity for a variety of types of love. Selfish at birth, we soon learn filial love for our parents.

Eros love, or physical attraction, comes along during our teen years.

Agape love, which gives freely yet expects nothing in return, is learned as we follow the example of Jesus. As Christians we can love every person God brings our way, though we may not agree with his or her actions.

When we are living within the Christian marriage contract, deep physical, mental, and spiritual union develops over the years. We discuss it more than we used to in society, but we emphasize the wrong aspects of it.

There is a vast difference between genuine physical union as the total sharing experience it should be in marriage and the sin-is-fun, sex-is-a-must, you-must-have-this-to-get-it mentality. A widow knows and understands this difference.

Many people don't! And so we must warn the new widow, "Don't be surprised when your best friend's husband (or your first date or even your brother-in-law) offers to go to bed with you. 'Just to help out and to relieve your tensions and frustrations so you can cope and keep going!' he may say."

Good physical union is not a momentary, temporary—and certainly not an isolated—act. Marriage partners grow into physical union a little like you'd put a jigsaw puzzle together, piece by piece, to finally obtain a colorful, complete picture.

Some of the pieces might include

. . . someone warm and cuddly beside you in bed each morning, many mornings.

. . . being adored without facial makeup.

. . . buying his brand of soap, toothpaste, or shaving cream.

. . . a first anniversary, a seventh, a twenty-fifth.

. . . an extended family with extra people to remember on holidays.

. . . counting pennies for a movie.

. . . tears of joy.

. . . the birth of a child, another, another.

. . . a footstep recognized and reacted to with happiness.

. . . a shouting argument; tension; making up.

. . . a bent fender on a new car and a Christian who said, "It's not eternal."

. . . gut-level conversation you've never shared before.

... a secure embrace after a nightmare.

... red roses you secretly hoped for after the first child, but which finally arrived after the fourth.

... a variety of ways of saying "I love you" and "I'm sorry."

... someone who telephones at four from work every day to see how you are.

... learning to interpret his emotions without any words being spoken.

... slides of faraway places and relaxed times together.

... two arms to enfold you when the breast lump is discovered, and the voice that assures, "It's all okay" when you are still groggy from surgery.

... discussion over the exact meaning of a Scripture verse.

... someone to check the house at night when you "heard something."

... a partner when you walk off excess calories in the park.

... sweaty headbands to wash with his man-sized clothes after tennis.

... a surprise, "What can I do to help you?" when you *really* need it.

... someone to complain to when the car falls apart.

... the ultimate earthly physical ecstacy and fulfillment of sexual intercourse after a gentle pat at six in the morning; a goodbye kiss at seven; a telephone call at four; a loving embrace at six; and several hints that you are still interesting and exciting in *all* ways to him—year after year after year.
THAT'S WHAT THE WIDOW MISSES...

It's when there's *no one* "besides you," and your eldest son graduates from high school in the upper ten percent; when your daughter presents you with your first grandson, and he looks like your dead husband; when you accomplish something and no one is home to share it; when your youngest begins to smile like his dad; when your daughter spends time with Grandfather and you are proud. Who do you share these times with?

It's the total loneliness that becomes nearly unbearable. That's when friends, relatives, Jesus, counselors, and all good listening ears begin the lengthy task of helping the widow work through grief and start to heal. Thanks for caring enough to try to do it well. I can't reward you, but Jesus will.

*"Begin now to read educational books
that are going to prove beneficial."*
—Comment made at a Solitaires meeting

Books

In closing, let me say that the Bible gave me strength and was the most helpful book to me after my husband's death. Lay people took me to teachers who explained it well. *Good Grief* by Westberg helped me most in understanding myself. *The Burden is Light* by Eugenia Price helped me see I could change. *Go, Man, Go!, God is Fabulous, Hot Line to Heaven,* and *Praise the Lord, Anyway* helped me have a positive attitude. James Kennedy's *Evangelism Explosion* helped me learn to talk about Jesus. *How to Live Like a King's Kid* by Harold Hill boosted me on.

Here are some comments from other widows:

"A pamphlet offered free that I obtained from a ladies' magazine on how to arrange funerals was the thing I had read in the past that helped me most."

"I mostly read the Bible, searching for something I thought maybe I had missed."

"I didn't read. Trying to put more information into a brain already full of cobwebs creates more havoc."

"Someone gave me Catherine Marshall's *To Live Again*. It's good anytime."

"*How to Tell Your Children about Death* was particularly helpful."

"I liked Helen Steiner Rice's inspirational verses, especially 'When I Must Leave You,' and notes of comfort from other widows."

"I enjoyed books by C. S. Lewis so much that I bought every one he wrote, for all ages."

"I've read and studied the stock market and about wills already. You can learn anything you need to know by reading it in books."

The women praised well-written books, especially testimonies and spiritual guidance books, and suggested, in addition to others already mentioned, the following:

Bayly, Joseph. *View from a Hearse*. Elgin, Ill.: David C. Cook Publishing Co., 1973.
Claypool, John. *Tracks of A Fellow Struggler*. Waco, Texas: Word Books, 1974.

Decker, Beatrice and Kooiman, Gladys. *After the Flowers Have Gone*. Grand Rapids: Zondervan, 1973.

Marshall, Catherine. *The Helper*. Carmel, New York: Guideposts, 1978.

Matthews, A. J. *Why Me?* Fort Washington, Pa.: Christian Literature Crusade, 1972.

Ozment, Robert V. *When Sorrow Comes*. Waco, Texas: Word Books, 1970.

Petersen, J. Alan. *For Families Only*. Wheaton, Ill.: Tyndale, 1977.

Taves, Isabella. *Love Must Not Be Wasted*. New York: Crowell, 1974.

Towns, James E. *Faith Stronger Than Death*. Anderson, Ind.: Warner Press, 1975.

Urch, Elizabeth. *Be Still My Soul*. Fort Washington, Pa.: Christian Literature Crusade, 1964.

Wold, Margaret. *The Critical Moment*. Minneapolis: Augsburg, 1978.

Young, Amy L. *By Death or Divorce . . . It Hurts to Lose*. Denver: Accent Books, 1976.

"I received the most help from *other widows*" is a statement with which many widows agree. That's one reason I began taking widows out to lunch, individually, and sharing. It's a pleasant way to follow biblical instructions.

Then Solitaires grew into a helpful group. This book, by help from the power of the Holy Spirit and a generous portion of human help from several of His family members, was brought into being from there.

Why don't you take a widow out to lunch?

DATE DUE

DEMCO 38-297